ICTs IN LIBRARIES

ICTs IN LIBRARY

Edited by
KUSUM VERMA

AKANSHA PUBLISHING HOUSE
NEW DELHI - 110 002 (INDIA)

AKANSHA PUBLISHING HOUSE
R-37B, Vani Vihar, Uttam Nagar
New Delhi-110 059
E-mail: ektabooks@yahoo.com

Showroom:
4649/21B, Ansari Road,
Daryaganj, New Delhi-110 002
Phone: 9212065579, 9811582579

ICTs in Libraries

First Published, 2004
Reprint 2012
ISBN 81-87606-75-4

PRINTED IN INDIA

Published by M.P. Misra for Akansha Publishing House, New Delhi-110 002 and Printed at Tarun Offset Press, Delhi.

Preface

The dawn of information revolution is considered to be one of the marvels of the twentieth century. The new technologies have not only transformed the shape of modem libraries but also created very many exciting possibilities and opportunities. The modern digital libraries are not only considered as centres for the creation and recreation of information product and services, but also as dynamic catalysts of research and development activities having a strong role to contribute significantly for achieving academic excellence in an organisation. This fact has brought a major shift to the responsibilities of the libraries not only to engage to house the collection, and provide routine services to the end users but also to generate financial resources for their respective institutions.

In addition to traditional text-based information, modern information systems are now able to represent the information electronically and to manipulate automatically at high speeds. Such information represented digitally, in two states, or binary form is often referred to as digital information. Magnetic tapes, magnetic disks and optical discs form the basic recording and storage media in digital forms. The capture of data for electronic storage and digital processing is accomplished by manual and automatic techniques. The rapid technological developments have made it clear that the familiar role of librarians as information intermediaries must undergo immense change, if the librarians are to avoid being displaced by a variety of contenders.

The role of information technology in modern libraries are described elaborately in the present volume. The opportunities and challenges of digitised libraries are also discussed. The work will serve as a highly beneficial reference tool to librarians, information scientists, researchers, students and teachers.

Editor

Contents

1

Electronic Libraries

The new electronic versions of established journals have not attracted much attention, and the new purely electronic journals are not deluged with submissions. The predictions of a shift towards electronic journals are multiplying, but no dramatic changes are visible yet. The gradual evolution towards electronic journals is not surprising. It is common for transition to a new technology to take many years. Even the compact disk took a decade to displace the vinyl disk. On the other hand, there are also many rosy predictions about rapid development of electronic commerce (ecommerce), with electronic shopping malls and intelligent software "agents" scouring the Net for the best deals for consumers.

The current situation and the future appear to be much more complicated. Online services have revenues in the billions of dollars. They do not use the Internet yet, but they might switch to it as their delivery vehicle. In any case, they provide a successful model of profitable electronic trade in information goods. So far, they are mostly restricted to certain professional services where their value is easily appreciated.

The complaints about not knowing how to make money on the Internet refer largely to the mass market. Many newspapers and magazines have electronic editions, but have not yet figured out how to make them profitable. There are frequent complaints that the lack of security on the Internet is what inhibits ecommerce. However, those security problems are likely to be solved soon through implementation of known cryptographic techniques.

In any case, these problems are much exaggerated, since current credit card payment systems are adequate for most purposes, even for Internet purchases. A more serious inhibition to the growth of ecommerce is probably the lack of convincing economic models of how to conduct it. Ecommerce is often predicted to promote "friction-free capitalism," in which various overhead and middlemen costs are eliminated.

Someone wishing to purchase a VCR might send an "intelligent agent" into the Internet to collect bids from suppliers for a unit that meets desired specifications, and then select the best choice. While such a vision will be feasible technically, it is extremely unlikely to be dominant. The general tendency in the marketplace is to avoid "commoditization," in which there are many almost equivalent products and services, and where price is the only consideration. Sometimes commoditization is hard to resist. Sometimes it is because consumers learn there is little to differentiate products.

As an example, oil companies have pretty much given up on trying to convince people that gasoline differs in anything other than octane ratings. In other cases, commoditization is forced on an industry by government edict or effective private monopoly. Intel and Microsoft have reduced the IBM-compatible PC industry to a commodity business, in which they collect almost all the profits, and the other players scramble to find a niche that will enable them to do more than just break even. However, those are the exceptions. The general ecological principle is towards evolution of species that fill different roles. Zebras do not attempt to compete with giraffes, but exploit a different part of the ecosystem, and evolution does not lead to a convergence of those two species.

Similarly, in the world of business, companies try to differentiate their products. Workstation producers could never in the past agree on a common version of Unix, even under the threat of being overwhelmed by PCs, since that would have required giving up the distinctive features that bound them to their customers. Even airlines, which are basically in the commodity business of moving people from one city to another, try to differentiate themselves through frequent flier plans and special pricing schemes. Ecommerce is likely to lead to a proliferation of pricing plans that will seem to most people to be much more frustrating and less rational than even today's U.S. airlines.

There will probably be a niche market for people who care most about their convenience, and will use their intelligent agents to do their shopping for them. Most of the Internet stores that sell CDs prevent software agents from collecting prices for comparison shopping. We can expect more such barriers. Trade on the Internet in information goods, such as movies, music, and scholarly publications, is likely to involve pricing and distribution schemes that will seem even further removed from the popular conception of a "just price." The reason is that with distribution costs negligible, only the "first copy" cost of creating a work will matter. This will create novel possibilities in the search for maximal profits.

Two of the most important factors that are likely to affect trade in information goods are bundling and differential pricing. Bundling consists of offering several goods together in a single package, such as combining a word processor, a spreadsheet, and a presentation program in a software suite, or else printing many stories in a single newspaper. When dealing with physical goods, bundling often makes intuitive sense, since there are obvious economies in production and distribution. The accepted wisdom is that ecommerce will lead to the electronic equivalent of just that, with readers selecting and paying for individual stories. Trade in information goods will have this same problem.

There will be high fixed costs, practically no incremental costs, and a uniform price will usually have to be set for all. Bundling can then be used to capture some of the "consumer surplus" by smoothing out the uneven preferences people have for different goods and services. Software suites such as Microsoft Office are just one example, as is the spread of site licensing of software packages. Internet service providers with flat access fees are growing much faster than traditional online service providers such as America on Line and Prodigy, which charge by the hour. Cable TV does not charge for each channel separately, but for packages of them.

Similarly, in software, where there is much talk about network computers that will download small applications, past experience with pay-per-use is discouraging, and suggests that micropayments will not play a major role. The other major factor that is likely to influence ecommerce. A producer of information goods would like to charge according to the consumer's willingness to pay, but the consumer will usually be reluctant to reveal such information. However, it is sometimes possible to correlate willingness to pay with other features. Airlines offer much cheaper tickets for those willing to be away from home on Saturday night, on the theory that business travelers, who are willing to pay a lot, will not be willing to put up with such inconvenience.

In information services, online services such as Prodigy and CompuServe offer stock market quotes that are delayed by 15 or 20 minutes for no extra cost, beyond the basic subscription. Real-time quotes uniformly cost extra, on the theory that those who need them for their trading will pay more. Electronic publications may offer high-resolution versions at one price, a lower-resolution version at a lower one, and sometimes they might offer a fax-quality version at no charge. There are already interesting experiments going on in book distribution, with authors making some parts of their manuscripts freely available on the Internet, to advertise their work, to update it with lists of current errata, and to make available features that draw on the unique capabilities of the electronic medium.

There are also likely to be differentials based on timeliness, as with stock market quotes; old issues might be offered at low or no charge. Such legislative protection is likely to be enacted, as the proposed changes in copyright laws would give copyright holders almost complete control over the usage of their works. While the Internet does offer ways to improve delivery of medical and legal services, we should not expect a decrease in demand for lawyers. They will have many new opportunities to exercise their trade. Many corporations report that monitoring software usage to comply with licensing terms costs just as much as the software itself.

There are systems under development for automatic tracking of licenses and fees, but the economic logic may militate against their use, and overheads associated with ecommerce may end up much higher than the ones we complain about right now in trade in physical goods. Although some publishers talk about attempting to attract individual subscribers, there is no evidence this is likely to succeed. On the other hand, there may be more extensive bundling by publishers, with journals being offered only in groups, which might at least temporarily gain an advantage for some publishers. Differential pricing has been a feature of scholarly publications for a long time, in that library subscription rates are almost uniformly several times higher than those for individuals.

Some journals provide free access only to older issues. There are even journals that provide free electronic access to current issues, while charging for print versions. It is not clear whether this is a viable strategy even in the intermediate term, since the availability of free electronic versions might lead to cuts in print subscriptions. The practice of making old issues of a subscription electronic journal available for free seems attractive. A major concern of scholars and librarians is the guaranteed availability of an electronic journal. When a library purchases a book or printed journal, it can keep it forever.

In general, scholarly journals have not as yet been significantly affected by electronic publications. Publishers are coping with decreasing circulations and increased publications volume by raising prices, and that is meeting increasing resistance. Few publishers have accepted the need to reduce their prices. Publishers are trying to maintain their old mode of operation for the print versions of their journals, with the old cost structure, and in addition produce an electronic version. There are possibilities for alleviating the cost pressures on publishers and libraries, at least for a while, which do not force publishers' revenues to drop. Only about one third of the costs of a typical research library is devoted to purchases of books and journals. If journals were to provide electronic versions not only of their current issues but also of old ones, libraries could dispense with their bound journal collections, and save at least one third of their costs, while maintaining their reference librarian staffs and paying the old prices.

However, that would be a drastic step that few scholars, librarians, or publishers seem ready for. It would have to be done on a large scale, and all affected institutions would have to be ready with equipment and training of their staff. Changes are more noticeable in corporate libraries, where it is common to find that spending on online information sources is far greater than on books and journals. One feature that many librarians are likely to find distasteful is that of providing their clients inferior data. This will be a reversal of their traditional roles of preserving and making as widely available as possible a variety of scholarly materials in the best form possible. If the prediction of extensive bundling and price differentiation in information goods that was made above comes to pass, though, libraries may end up as agents of publishers in limiting the ease of use of data.

While librarians do not think of themselves as providers of inferior data, to a large extent that is what they have been since the beginning. Personal possession of a book is usually far superior to borrowing a copy from the library. That is largely what allowed libraries to coexist with bookstores. For publishers of fiction, libraries help in segmenting the market, charging different prices to different users, and thus maximizing revenues. Libraries coexist with this system, since to use library copies, patrons have to put up with the inconvenience of waiting for their turn on the reservation list, going to the library to pick up the book, having to read it in just a week or two, and so on.

Thus libraries serve a different segment of the market than bookstores. In comparison, the total revenue of all publishers in the world from mathematics journals is around $200 million per year. Publishers are only slowly coming to the realization that their traditional role as the main disseminators of information is rapidly becoming obsolete. Scholars are able to dispense with the publishers' functions in disseminating conventional publications at only a slight increase in the scholars' own work. To maintain their revenues, publishers will need to switch to providing new value-added services that are becoming possible in the digital world, such as animated multimedia versions of papers.

The main problem is that scholars have more and more opportunities and temptations to bypass traditional publishers. It is possible to have a thriving commercial business distributing freely available information. Free electronic journals have shown that it is possible to have high editorial and refereeing standards in an electronic format, together with various novel features, such as animation and forward referencing, which are possible only in the digital world. Full use of the novel features of electronic publishing, such as multimedia presentation, requires new skills and substantial effort.

The one advantage of electronic journals that is cited most often, namely faster publication, appears to be unimportant. Most scholarly articles are read by a few other experts, and authors are able to reach those experts through electronic preprint distribution. The perverse economic incentives that led to the growth of the present unwieldy and expensive scholarly journal industry are leading to an unstable situation. Authors have never had to consider the costs that their decisions on where to publish caused for the entire community, since those costs were spread so widely. There are examples where large communities shifted from reliance on inexpensive journals that were supported partially through page charges towards much more expensive journals that did not force the authors to pay anything towards publishing their works.

Scholars have never been asked to make tradeoffs. Moreover, in several institutions, when they were asked whether they were willing to give up journals, they have said no. That response is not surprising, though, since they were not offered anything in return for the cancellation of subscriptions. Publishers claim that their traditional journals provide an important service by validating research results through the refereeing process, and certifying the quality of what they publish. However, free electronic journals have proved they can provide these services as well, and at much lower cost. Even more important, this validation and certification are "common goods" that no individual institution any longer has a strong incentive to pay for.

For the validation and certification process to function, it would be enough to have one copy of the journal in the world. Even established journals are losing circulation, and many of the new journals have distressingly low subscription lists. For new journals, commercial publishers in many fields regard 300 paid subscriptions as a success. This is a small number, and surely some authors would be upset if they knew their work was only going to be available in that many libraries. Scholars can distribute their work in preprint form to all the experts they wish to alert to their work, and now through preprint servers and home pages on the Web they increasingly make their work available to everyone in the world. Scholars are increasingly insisting on the right to continue distributing their preprints even after publication of their work in a journal.

When a large professional society proposed a revision of its copyright policy that would have explicitly limited this right, it was faced with a revolt by its editors and authors and had to back down. The advantages of free electronic distribution are such that an increasing number of scholars are relying primarily on Internet access for keeping up with their fields. Library budgets have been increasing rapidly. The frequent complaints about cutbacks have mostly reflected cuts in the number of journal subscriptions. Budgets have gone down only on rare occasions. However, even rapid library budget increases have not been sufficient to keep up with rises in journal costs. Some universities are beginning to make substantial changes in their library policies, such as using document delivery services on a massive scale to substitute for journal subscriptions.

The economics of scholarly journal publishing make such moves economically attractive to libraries, and disastrous to publishers. Publishers could try to respond by increasing their copyright fees, but that would only create increased incentives for authors to use preprints to bypass the journals. Librarians may or may not have "unexpended funds." Publishers' revenues come from sales of products to, or the right to use the product by, customers. Products may include books, journals and other serials, audiovisual materials, and electronic publications. Journal revenues may be based primarily on subscriptions, with or without advertising, or journals may be distributed to readers at no cost but be fully subsidized by the advertisers.

Most scholarly journals are subscription based, and that is the model considered here. On average, subscription-based journals derive about 75% of their revenues from subscriptions, with 15% coming from advertising, 3% from the page and submissions fees charged by some journals, and the balance of 7% from miscellaneous other revenues, including author reprints, copyright fees and individual copy sales. Copyright administration and rights sales may include user fees, on-line fees or copying fees for journals, as well as subsidiary, translation, paperback and broadcast/film or magazine serialization rights for books. Some university presses and scholarly societies also receive funds or subsidies from universities, grants and foundations and/or membership dues.

Publishers lose sales revenues and licensing income when their publications are extensively photocopied without reimbursement, or when used books are resold, or when books are pirated abroad. New publications may take time to get established. Sales of older, backlist publications—especially books--diminish over time. Indeed, the sales curve for virtually all publications begins to decline long before backlisting, which usually occurs a year after publication. Over all, more than half of all books published lose money. For journals, it is more common now than in the past that some journals publish at a loss, and even journals that are eventually profitable can take as long as five years to reach profitability.

Books and journals that lose money are subsidized by other sources or products, and this has led some publishers to publish more books to spread the risk--a strategy that has not always paid off. Publishers' expectations differ as to how soon a publication should pay for itself, break even and generate income in excess of costs. Scholarly and professional publishers commonly set their prices based on a mix of factors, such as the prices of competing products, the size of the potential market, the mix of distribution channels, their assumptions about how many copies or subscriptions they will sell, their projected costs and need for income to invest in new programs. Usually each new book is treated as a separate project, expected to pay for itself and then make a profit in its first and sometimes only printing over a relatively short time span.

In contrast, high level textbooks for professionals or scholars in training, and reference works, tend to have a flatter, shorter curve in relation to anticipated new editions, which are more predictable over time. As scholars and researchers have become increasingly specialized over the last three decades, dividing into smaller and smaller "niche" groups, the number of potential readers for any given treatise has declined. At the same time a growing population of researchers and scholars of all types who seek to publish their research has increased the number of monographs submitted to publishers. New journals and large reference book projects usually take some years to reach profitable sales levels. Continuing projects such as these tend to develop a consistent sales history over time that makes it somewhat easier to estimate the number of subscribers and the resulting revenue stream.

Publishers and professional associations frequently use profits from other projects to underwrite the costs of a new journal for a period of as long as five years, until the break-even point is reached. These development costs often clash with the irresistible market forces of price sensitivity. Some new methods of manuscript preparation and production may even require more steps and/or personnel. To impose a statistical perspective, if a monograph publisher saved 10% on production costs by automating pre-print activities, and production costs accounted for 30% of the total costs of publishing the monograph, then the overall savings for that monograph would be 3%—not a material cost savings.

If publishers produce books and journals on line, once again the cost will decrease only slightly because most of the cost is incurred "up front." Similarly, if librarians and end users "purchase" on-line books only when they print out pages at their local PC, those few pages printed out will have to carry the full burden of the costs of getting all the material on line at the pre-printing stage. It would seem to follow that the price per page in this scenario would grow exponentially, and probably extend well beyond the financial resources of individual purchasers.

A commercial press is accountable to the owner of the business, whether that is an individual, association, institution or group of shareholders. Its officers are accountable for a fair rate of return on investment, which is defined in various ways, but at the minimum should be greater than investors would get if they put their money into a bank. Like other large corporate entities, publicly held publishers are also under pressure to deliver favorable returns on a quarterly basis.

University presses are accountable to their universities and boards of trustees. It is often assumed that university presses are accountable to their faculties to publish their works, but few university presses have more than a third of their authors from their own institutions, and the largest ones have even fewer. While university presses are "not-for-profit" for tax purposes, this does not mean that they manage their business to "break even." The larger university presses are asked to provide income or "contributions" to their sponsoring institutions, and that trend is growing among medium sized university presses as well. University presses usually must find their own funding to invest in new products.

More and more universities are unwilling to subsidize the presses that lose money, although many indirect subsidies can occur in a campus setting. Scholarly societies are accountable to their members, and along lines similar to the university presses. They are more likely than for-profit publishers to charge authors a per page fee to publish, a part of the revenue "mix" that allows societies to offer their members special, lower subscription prices.

Publications of the learned societies may account for up to seventy percent of the societies' revenues, with meetings and conferences the second large piece and membership dues a small percentage of the total income. Society publishers are especially accountable to providing their members with a price benefit for their publications. This is one of the factors that has led to multi-tiered pricing for individual and institutional subscribers.

All publishers are accountable to their authors and their customers and, in a different way, to their employees and suppliers. Publishers need to do a good job for their authors, to present their information fairly, accurately, effectively and attractively, and to market their work well. Failure to do so results in disgruntled authors, who can ruin a publisher's reputation in the marketplace. Thus there is a parallel between the need for publishers to satisfy their authors and the need for librarians to satisfy their faculties, just as there is a parallel between the need for publishers to satisfy their customers and librarians to satisfy their readers.

The publisher's perceived visibility and status in the marketplace influences the scholar's or researcher's perceived status. Effective marketing leads to high visibility and happy authors. Publishers are accountable to customers for the quality of their products, for informing customers, including secondary publishers, about product content, price and availability, and for timely and cost effective delivery in good condition.

When the customers are bookstores, wholesalers or subscription agents, the publisher develops a marketing partnership with the bookseller to reach the end-user. Long-term success depends on profitable growth. This means selling more units of each book or journal title, constantly improving the sales of the top titles while publishing fewer that drain the fiscal resources of the company. A good balance of providing customers with the information they need and providing investors with a fair return on investment is the key to success.

Sound financial management that improves profitability through a positive price:cost ratio also helps publishers continue to produce the return expected by their owners. Timing, adaptability and sufficient capital are key risk/survival/ success issues in the rapidly changing environment. These realities pertain both to commercial publishers and to the not-for-profits. Although they may measure financial results differently, they face the same constraints, restrictions and expectations. This point needs to be emphasized and repeated.

University librarians have noted that both they and end users may well have only very partial ideas of publishers' cost factors in scholarly publication. Professional and scholarly publishers, who have long been aware of budget constraints in library purchases of print materials, want to know more about the trends of economic measures relating to libraries generally, and in relation to their scientific, technical and medical collections and services. Allocations for library materials and collections are around thirty percent, and general and administrative costs, equipment, communications services and preservation take more of the library's budget.

In United States, the cost of materials, though only one portion of a library's overall budget, has attracted much attention. With high fixed costs for other budgetary items, the variable cost of material expenditures takes on even more attention. With spiraling costs for some journals and tense relations between publishers and librarians, the search for alternatives is intense, and current journal pricing is perceived as a bottleneck—this bottleneck must also include the price placed on intellectual property and its protection. Elimination of local holdings for economic or other reasons creates a bottleneck of accessibility by traditional methods.

Eliminating or postponing the purchase of scholarly monographs in order to maintain journals collections. This option has been so widely exercised over the last two decades that the market for and publication of scholarly monographs has dramatically declined. Providing access to the information through increased interlibrary loans and/or the use of commercial document delivery services, through resource sharing among a group of collaborative libraries, or through licensing of electronic access and transmission of information on local or wide area networks.

Systems and policies are still in their infancy, as both librarians and publishers hope that collaborative studies of technology and usage, some of them already in progress, will answer the many technical and economic questions surrounding setting up new ways to price information. Seeking additional funding from government and private sector grants, from endowments and gift funds, and from revenue generating activities, such additional funds to be used for the purchase of materials.

Libraries have not to date preferred this option because increasing competition among higher education institutions for such funds means that libraries cannot count on higher levels of income from such sources. An interesting productivity and personnel trend is that public service functions are requiring more skilled, professional staff as technical services functions shift more to support staff or are even outsourced. While two-thirds of a university library's employees may have consisted of non-professional support staff, there has traditionally been little turnover in these positions and great resistance to change.

In public universities support staff are likely to be civil service and/or unionized employees. Yet, as in most industries, the lower level and less skilled jobs have been eliminated more rapidly than high skilled or professional jobs. Allocations for automation, including capital investment in computers and other equipment, are increasing more rapidly than any other budget area. Automation costs today may represent up to twenty-five percent of the total library budget. This allocation includes services from groups such as OCLC or intra-institutional groups such as a university computer center. Finally, there is a steady five to ten percent of costs associated with administration, including staff training.

Librarians have many masters. They may be accountable to university administrators, faculty, boards, donors and—in the case of public universities—legislators. Libraries' financial accountability to university administrators or their governing boards is to stay within budget and to manage their funds reasonably and effectively. The quality of a university library's collection and services is central to the faculty's teaching and research. The faculty are a powerful constituency and at some universities decide how the library's materials budget is spent.

In other institutions, librarians make purchasing decisions, but usually with significant faculty input. Reporting may occur to various governing boards of the library and the university, and to the governing boards of regional and national accrediting and standards agencies. University libraries may be accountable to legislatures and/or private donors to ensure that money has been well spent. Donors and foundations also often have interests and expectations concerning the excellence, reputation and quality of the institution, and may require acknowledgment in the form of the naming of buildings or collections or in other forms of public recognition.

Students are the largest group of other stakeholders, with marked influence on library hours, study space and service allocations. Many students, and generally the parents of students, may be more interested in the libraries' technological capabilities and collections. Alumni have expectations regarding the prestige of their university libraries and the maintenance of traditional collections, and they too look for access to library collections and new technology. Local community taxpayers also want access and expect "more for less" in relation to the taxes they are willing to pay. Consortial colleagues expect prompt response to interlibrary loan requests and, increasingly, collaborative involvement in networked information and shared resources agreements.

The professional community of librarians looks to university librarians to provide leadership in special projects, especially in preservation, new technology and cooperative resource development. Managing budgets well and educating the stakeholders to perceive libraries and their services as essential to the institution are key survival skills for library executives. Effective public relations, communication and information on library services is part of this educational outreach. Libraries today also need to develop credibility in delivering services efficiently and to be proactive in providing new services that other institutions or departments cannot or do not provide.

Librarians need to anticipate customer needs—for example, archiving of electronic materials. The benefits of electronic publishing include increased speed of publication and ease of soliciting user feedback, which can be incorporated into or tagged to appearnext to the original work. Electronic publication provides the potential for reinventing traditional peer review by making it practical for subscribers to volunteer their services as reviewers. Even when the final product is a print publication, electronic technology for editing and production functions, e.g. capturing authors' keystrokes, editing on-line or on disk, typesetting, and producing/printing/duplicating/copying information, may ease production, require less labor and reduce costs in the production process.

Similarly, electronic production requires personnel with a large amount of training in many technical fields, probably better trained and better paid than the personnel required for traditional print publishing. Electronic information is potentially easy to change, use and publish in a wide variety of formats. It offers extraordinary opportunities for developing new kinds of searching engines, both within an original work and at the library level. Obsolescence and technological advancement are, however, issues which must be considered in evaluating the economics of electronic storage.

As an alternative to physical storage, electronic storage becomes one answer to the question of where the archiving and preservation of the scholarly tradition should occur. Another possibility is that libraries might develop collaborative contracts with publishers, by which the publishers maintain the archive of their own publications. Some characteristics of electronic publishing are more ambiguous. This ambiguity can stem from several factors: the number of potential "self-publishers" with access to networks, the interactive nature of certain electronic forms, the potentially public, i.e. networked, nature of many of the steps in the publishing process, e.g. peer review and commentary.

In short, in an electronic environment, the authorship, identity and ownership of a work can become less clear because of the collaborative efforts to create it and the multiple inputs to construct it. The digital environment means that every copy is a technological equal of the original.

Role of E-publishers

Most major publishers have big electronic ventures, and some now offer all their journals in electronic formats. Within half a dozen years, practically all current publications are likely to be available in electronic form. There is rapid proliferation of electronic scholarly journals. The ARL survey [ARL] found 74 peer-reviewed electronic journals at the beginning of 1994, and 142 a year later. By now, this number is bound to be several times higher, since many established print journals have come out with electronic versions in the last year, whereas the 1994 ARL list included primarily journals that had been founded in electronic format only. However, even 1,000 electronic journals would be a tiny fraction of all refereed scholarly journals. Therefore, as far as most scholars are concerned, not much has changed.

Most journal articles that they read come from printed issues, and most submissions for publication are intended for traditional journals. The new electronic versions of established journals have not attracted much attention, and the new purely electronic journals are not deluged with submissions. The predictions of a shift towards electronic journals are multiplying, but no dramatic changes are visible yet. The gradual evolution towards electronic journals is not surprising. It is common for transition to a new technology to take many years. Even the compact disk took a decade to displace the vinyl disk.

On the other hand, there are also many rosy predictions about rapid development of electronic commerce (ecommerce), with electronic shopping malls and intelligent software "agents" scouring the Net for the best deals for consumers. The current situation and the future appear to be much more complicated. Online services have revenues in the billions of dollars. They do not use the Internet yet, but they might switch to it as their delivery vehicle. In any case, they provide a successful model of profitable electronic trade in information goods. So far, they are mostly restricted to certain professional services where their value is easily appreciated. The complaints about not knowing how to make money on the Internet refer largely to the mass market.

Many newspapers and magazines have electronic editions, but have not yet figured out how to make them profitable. There are frequent complaints that the lack of security on the Internet is what inhibits ecommerce. However, those security problems are likely to be solved soon through implementation of known cryptographic techniques. In any case, these problems are much exaggerated, since current credit card payment systems are adequate for most purposes, even for Internet purchases.

A more serious inhibition to the growth of ecommerce is probably the lack of convincing economic models of how to conduct it. Ecommerce is often predicted to promote "friction-free capitalism," in which various overhead and middlemen costs are eliminated. Someone wishing to purchase a VCR might send an "intelligent agent" into the Internet to collect bids from suppliers for a unit that meets desired specifications, and then select the best choice. While such a vision will be feasible technically, it is extremely unlikely to be dominant.

The general tendency in the marketplace is to avoid "commoditization," in which there are many almost equivalent products and services, and where price is the only consideration. Sometimes commoditization is hard to resist. Sometimes it is because consumers learn there is little to differentiate products. As an example, oil companies have pretty much given up on trying to convince people that gasoline differs in anything other than octane ratings. In other cases, commoditization is forced on an industry by government edict or effective private monopoly. Intel and Microsoft have reduced the IBM-compatible PC industry to a commodity business, in which they collect almost all the profits, and the other players scramble to find a niche that will enable them to do more than just break even. However, those are the exceptions.

The general ecological principle is towards evolution of species that fill different roles. Zebras do not attempt to compete with giraffes, but exploit a different part of the ecosystem, and evolution does not lead to a convergence of those two species. Similarly, in the world of business, companies try to differentiate their products. Workstation producers could never in the past agree on a common version of Unix, even under the threat of being overwhelmed by PCs, since that would have required giving up the distinctive features that bound them to their customers.

Even airlines, which are basically in the commodity business of moving people from one city to another, try to differentiate themselves through frequent flier plans and special pricing schemes. Ecommerce is likely to lead to a proliferation of pricing plans that will seem to most people to be much more frustrating and less rational than even today's U.S. airlines. There will probably be a niche market for people who care most about their convenience, and will use their intelligent agents to do their shopping for them. Most of the Internet stores that sell CDs prevent software agents from collecting prices for comparison shopping. We can expect more such barriers.

Trade on the Internet in information goods, such as movies, music, and scholarly publications, is likely to involve pricing and distribution schemes that will seem even further removed from the popular conception of a "just price." The reason is that with distribution costs negligible, only the "first copy" cost of creating a work will matter. This will create novel possibilities in the search for maximal profits. Two of the most important factors that are likely to affect trade in information goods are bundling and differential pricing. Bundling consists of offering several goods together in a single package, such as combining a word processor, a spreadsheet, and a presentation p:ogram in a software suite, or else printing many stories in a single newspaper.

When dealing with physical goods, bundling often makes intuitive sense, since there are obvious economies in production and distribution. The accepted wisdom is that ecommerce will lead to the electronic equivalent of just that, with readers selecting and paying for individual stories. Trade in information goods will have this same problem. There will be high fixed costs, practically no incremental costs, and a uniform price will usually have to be set for all. Bundling can then be used to capture some of the "consumer surplus" by smoothing out the uneven preferences people have for different goods and services. Software suites such as Microsoft Office are just one example, as is the spread of site licensing of software packages.

Internet service providers with flat access fees are growing much faster than traditional online service providers such as America on Line and Prodigy, which charge by the hour. Cable TV does not charge for each channel separately, but for packages of them. Similarly, in software, where there is much talk about network computers that will download small applications, past experience with pay-per-use is discouraging, and suggests that micropayments will not play a major role. The other major factor that is likely to influence ecommerce. A producer of information goods would like to charge according to the consumer's willingness to pay, but the consumer will usually be reluctant to reveal such information.

However, it is sometimes possible to correlate willingness to pay with other features. Airlines offer much cheaper tickets for those willing to be away from home on Saturday night, on the theory that business travelers, who are willing to pay a lot, will not be willing to put up with such inconvenience. In information services, online services such as Prodigy and CompuServe offer stock market quotes that are delayed by 15 or 20 minutes for no extra cost, beyond the basic subscription. Real-time quotes uniformly cost extra, on the theory that those who need them for their trading will pay more.

Electronic publications may offer high-resolution versions at one price, a lower-resolution version at a lower one, and sometimes they might offer a fax-quality version at no charge.

There are already interesting experiments going on in book distribution, with authors making some parts of their manuscripts freely available on the Internet, to advertise their work, to update it with lists of current errata, and to make available features that draw on the unique capabilities of the electronic medium. There are also likely to be differentials based on timeliness, as with stock market quotes; old issues might be offered at low or no charge. Such legislative protection is likely to be enacted, as the proposed changes in copyright laws would give copyright holders almost complete control over the usage of their works.

While the Internet does offer ways to improve delivery of medical and legal services, we should not expect a decrease in demand for lawyers. They will have many new opportunities to exercise their trade. Many corporations report that monitoring software usage to comply with licensing terms costs just as much as the software itself. There are systems under development for automatic tracking of licenses and fees, but the economic logic may militate against their use, and overheads associated with ecommerce may end up much higher than the ones we complain about right now in trade in physical goods. Although some publishers talk about attempting to attract individual subscribers, there is no evidence this is likely to succeed.

On the other hand, there may be more extensive bundling by publishers, with journals being offered only in groups, which might at least temporarily gain an advantage for some publishers. Differential pricing has been a feature of scholarly publications for a long time, in that library subscription rates are almost uniformly several times higher than those for individuals. Some journals provide free access only to older issues. There are even journals that provide free electronic access to current issues, while charging for print versions. It is not clear whether this is a viable strategy even in the intermediate term, since the availability of free electronic versions might lead to cuts in print subscriptions.

The practice of making old issues of a subscription electronic journal available for free seems attractive. A major concern of scholars and librarians is the guaranteed availability of an electronic journal. When a library purchases a book or printed journal, it can keep it forever. In general, scholarly journals have not as yet been significantly affected by electronic publications. Publishers are coping with decreasing circulations and increased publications volume by raising prices, and that is meeting increasing resistance.

Few publishers have accepted the need to reduce their prices. Publishers are trying to maintain their old mode of operation for the print versions of their journals, with the old cost structure, and in addition produce an electronic version. There are possibilities for alleviating the cost pressures on publishers and libraries, at least for a while, which do not force publishers' revenues to drop. Only about one third of the costs of a typical research library is devoted to purchases of books and journals.

If journals were to provide electronic versions not only of their current issues but also of old ones, libraries could dispense with their bound journal collections, and save at least one third of their costs, while maintaining their reference librarian staffs and paying the old prices. However, that would be a drastic step that few scholars, librarians, or publishers seem ready for. It would have to be done on a large scale, and all affected institutions would have to be ready with equipment and training of their staff. Changes are more noticeable in corporate libraries, where it is common to find that spending on online information sources is far greater than on books and journals. One feature that many librarians are likely to find distasteful is that of providing their clients inferior data. This will be a reversal of their traditional roles of preserving and making as widely available as possible a variety of scholarly materials in the best form possible.

If the prediction of extensive bundling and price differentiation in information goods that was made above comes to pass, though, libraries may end up as agents of publishers in limiting the ease of use of data. While librarians do not think of themselves as providers of inferior data, to a large extent that is what they have been since the beginning. Personal possession of a book is usually far superior to borrowing a copy from the library. That is largely what allowed libraries to coexist with bookstores.

For publishers of fiction, libraries help in segmenting the market, charging different prices to different users, and thus maximizing revenues. Libraries coexist with this system, since to use library copies, patrons have to put up with the inconvenience of waiting for their turn on the reservation list, going to the library to pick up the book, having to read it in just a week or two, and so on. Thus libraries serve a different segment of the market than bookstores. In comparison, the total revenue of all publishers in the world from mathematics journals is around $200 million per year. Publishers are only slowly coming to the realization that their traditional role as the main disseminators of information is rapidly becoming obsolete.

Scholars are able to dispense with the publishers' functions in disseminating conventional publications at only a slight increase in the scholars' own work. To maintain their revenues, publishers will need to switch to providing new value-added services that are becoming possible in the digital world, such as animated multimedia versions of papers. The main problem is that scholars have more and more opportunities and temptations to bypass traditional publishers. It is possible to have a thriving commercial business distributing freely available information.

Free electronic journals have shown that it is possible to have high editorial and refereeing standards in an electronic format, together with various novel features, such as animation and forward referencing, which are possible only in the digital world. Full use of the novel features of electronic publishing, such as multimedia presentation, requires new skills and substantial effort. The one advantage of electronic journals that is cited most often, namely faster publication, appears to be unimportant.

Most scholarly articles are read by a few other experts, and authors are able to reach those experts through electronic preprint distribution. The perverse economic incentives that led to the growth of the present unwieldy and expensive scholarly journal industry are leading to an unstable situation. Authors have never had to consider the costs that their decisions on where to publish caused for the entire community, since those costs were spread so widely. There are examples where large communities shifted from reliance on inexpensive journals that were supported partially through page charges towards much more expensive journals that did not force the authors to pay anything towards publishing their works. Scholars have never been asked to make tradeoffs. Moreover, in several institutions, when they were asked whether they were willing to give up journals, they have said no.

That response is not surprising, though, since they were not offered anything in return for the cancellation of subscriptions. Publishers claim that their traditional journals provide an important service by validating research results through the refereeing process, and certifying the quality of what they publish. However, free electronic journals have proved they can provide these services as well, and at much lower cost. Even more important, this validation and certification are "common goods" that no individual institution any longer has a strong incentive to pay for. For the validation and certification process to function, it would be enough to have one copy of the journal in the world.

Even established journals are losing circulation, and many of the new journals have distressingly low subscription lists. For new journals, commercial publishers in many fields regard 300 paid subscriptions as a success. This is a small number, and surely some authors would be upset if they knew their work was only going to be available in that many libraries. Scholars can distribute their work in preprint form to all the experts they wish to alert to their work, and now through preprint servers and home pages on the Web they increasingly make their work available to everyone in the world.

Scholars are increasingly insisting on the right to continue distributing their preprints even after publication of their work in a journal. When a large professional society proposed a revision of its copyright policy that would have explicitly limited this right, it was faced with a revolt by its editors and authors and had to back down. The advantages of free electronic distribution are such that an increasing number of scholars are relying primarily on Internet access for keeping up with their fields. Library budgets have been increasing rapidly. The frequent complaints about cutbacks have mostly reflected cuts in the number of journal subscriptions. Budgets have gone down only on rare occasions.

However, even rapid library budget increases have not been sufficient to keep up with rises in journal costs. Some universities are beginning to make substantial changes in their library policies, such as using document delivery services on a massive scale to substitute for journal subscriptions. The economics of scholarly journal publishing make such moves economically attractive to libraries, and disastrous to publishers. Publishers could try to respond by increasing their copyright fees, but that would only create increased incentives for authors to use preprints to bypass the journals.

Librarians may or may not have "unexpended funds." Publishers' revenues come from sales of products to, or the right to use the product by, customers. Products may include books, journals and other serials, audiovisual materials, and electronic publications. Journal revenues may be based primarily on subscriptions, with or without advertising, or journals may be distributed to readers at no cost but be fully subsidized by the advertisers. Most scholarly journals are subscription based, and that is the model considered here. On average, subscription-based journals derive about 75% of their revenues from subscriptions, with 15% coming from advertising, 3% from the page and submissions fees charged by some journals, and the balance of 7% from miscellaneous other revenues, including author reprints, copyright fees and individual copy sales.

Copyright administration and rights sales may include user fees, on-line fees or copying fees for journals, as well as subsidiary, translation, paperback and broadcast/film or magazine serialization rights for books. Some university presses and scholarly societies also receive funds or subsidies from universities, grants and foundations and/or membership dues. Publishers lose sales revenues and licensing income when their publications are extensively photocopied without reimbursement, or when used books are resold, or when books are pirated abroad. New publications may take time to get established. Sales of older, backlist publications—especially books--diminish over time.

Indeed, the sales curve for virtually all publications begins to decline long before backlisting, which usually occurs a year after publication. Over all, more than half of all books published lose money. For journals, it is more common now than in the past that some journals publish at a loss, and even journals that are eventually profitable can take as long as five years to reach profitability. Predicting which ones will reach their sales and profit goals, and which will not, is very difficult, if not impossible. Books and journals that lose money are subsidized by other sources or products, and this has led some publishers to publish more books to spread the risk--a strategy that has not always paid off.

Publishers' expectations differ as to how soon a publication should pay for itself, break even and generate income in excess of costs. Scholarly and professional publishers commonly set their prices based on a mix of factors, such as the prices of competing products, the size of the potential market, the mix of distribution channels, their assumptions about how many copies or subscriptions they will sell, their projected costs and need for income to invest in new programs.

Usually each new book is treated as a separate project, expected to pay for itself and then make a profit in its first and sometimes only printing over a relatively short time span. In contrast, high level textbooks for professionals or scholars in training, and reference works, tend to have a flatter, shorter curve in relation to anticipated new editions, which are more predictable over time. As scholars and researchers have become increasingly specialized over the last three decades, dividing into smaller and smaller "niche" groups, the number of potential readers for any given treatise has declined. At the same time a growing population of researchers and scholars of all types who seek to publish their research has increased the number of monographs submitted to publishers.

New journals and large reference book projects usually take some years to reach profitable sales levels. Continuing projects such as these tend to develop a consistent sales history over time that makes it somewhat easier to estimate the number of subscribers and the resulting revenue stream. Publishers and professional associations frequently use profits from other projects to underwrite the costs of a new journal for a period of as long as five years, until the break-even point is reached. These development costs often clash with the irresistible market forces of price sensitivity.

Some new methods of manuscript preparation and production may even require more steps and/or personnel. To impose a statistical perspective, if a monograph publisher saved 10% on production costs by automating pre-print activities, and production costs accounted for 30% of the total costs of publishing the monograph, then the overall savings for that monograph would be 3%—not a material cost savings. If publishers produce books and journals on line, once again the cost will decrease only slightly because most of the cost is incurred "up front."

Similarly, if librarians and end users "purchase" on-line books only when they print out pages at their local PC, those few pages printed out will have to carry the full burden of the costs of getting all the material on line at the pre-printing stage. It would seem to follow that the price per page in this scenario would grow exponentially, and probably extend well beyond the financial resources of individual purchasers. What is so far unknown is whether usage over time would increase sufficiently to spread the costs over a larger number of PC-printed "units." Thus, it is interesting that an internal study conducted at AT&T showed that demand for internally generated technical documents ebbed within a year after publication, until information about them was provided at the researchers' desktop computers.

Then demand extended to material five years old and beyond. This could have interesting implications for publishers' markets and pricing structures. A commercial press is accountable to the owner of the business, whether that is an individual, association, institution or group of shareholders. Its officers are accountable for a fair rate of return on investment, which is defined in various ways, but at the minimum should be greater than investors would get if they put their money into a bank. In today's business climate, many shareholders of large publishing corporations look for a return of 10% - 14% on their stock investment, consisting of a combination of the appreciation of the price of the stock and its paid dividends.

Like other large corporate entities, publicly held publishers are also under pressure to deliver favorable returns on a quarterly basis. University presses are accountable to their universities and boards of trustees. It is often assumed that university presses are accountable to their faculties to publish their works, but few university presses have more than a third of their authors from their own institutions, and the largest ones have even fewer. While university presses are "not-for-profit" for tax purposes, this does not mean that they manage their business to "break even."

The larger university presses are asked to provide income or "contributions" to their sponsoring institutions, and that trend is growing among medium sized university presses as well. University presses usually must find their own funding to invest in new products. More and more universities are unwilling to subsidize the presses that lose money, although many indirect subsidies can occur in a campus setting. Scholarly societies are accountable to their members, and along lines similar to the university presses. They are more likely than for-profit publishers to charge authors a per page fee to publish, a part of the revenue "mix" that allows societies to offer their members special, lower subscription prices. Publications of the learned societies may account for up to seventy percent of the societies' revenues, with meetings and conferences the second large piece and membership dues a small percentage of the total income.

Society publishers are especially accountable to providing their members with a price benefit for their publications. This is one of the factors that has led to multi-tiered pricing for individual and institutional subscribers. All publishers are accountable to their authors and their customers and, in a different way, to their employees and suppliers. Publishers need to do a good job for their authors, to present their information fairly, accurately, effectively and attractively, and to market their work well. Failure to do so results in disgruntled authors, who can ruin a publisher's reputation in the marketplace.

Thus there is a parallel between the need for publishers to satisfy their authors and the need for librarians to satisfy their faculties, just as there is a parallel between the need for publishers to satisfy their customers and librarians to satisfy their readers. The publisher's perceived visibility and status in the marketplace influences the scholar's or researcher's perceived status. Effective marketing leads to high visibility and happy authors. Publishers are accountable to customers for the quality of their products, for informing customers, including secondary publishers, about product content, price and availability, and for timely and cost effective delivery in good condition. When the customers are bookstores, wholesalers or subscription agents, the publisher develops a marketing partnership with the bookseller to reach the end-user.

Long-term success depends on profitable growth. This means selling more units of each book or journal title, constantly improving the sales of the top titles while publishing fewer that drain the fiscal resources of the company. A good balance of providing customers with the information they need and providing investors with a fair return on investment is the key to success. Sound financial management that improves profitability through a positive price:cost ratio also helps publishers continue to produce the return expected by their owners. Timing, adaptability and sufficient capital are key risk/survival/success issues in the rapidly changing environment. These realities pertain both to commercial publishers and to the not-for-profits.

Although they may measure financial results differently, they face the same constraints, restrictions and expectations. This point needs to be emphasized and repeated. Archiving of information preserves the records of culture and scholarship, as well as the preservation and/or conservation of artifact, providing housing for collections; shelving and organizing improve access for scholars; making decisions about what to preserve for future generations of scholars helps to shape our cultural heritage.

University librarians have noted that both they and end users may well have only very partial ideas of publishers' cost factors in scholarly publication. Professional and scholarly publishers, who have long been aware of budget constraints in library purchases of print materials, want to know more about the trends of economic measures relating to libraries generally, and in relation to their scientific, technical and medical collections and services. Allocations for library materials and collections are around thirty percent, and general and administrative costs, equipment, communications services and preservation take more of the library's budget. In United States, the cost of materials, though only one portion of a library's overall budget, has attracted much attention.

With high fixed costs for other budgetary items, the variable cost of material expenditures takes on even more attention. With spiraling costs for some journals and tense relations between publishers and librarians, the search for alternatives is intense, and current journal pricing is perceived as a bottleneck—this bottleneck must also include the price placed on intellectual property and its protection. Elimination of local holdings for economic or other reasons creates a bottleneck of accessibility by traditional methods. Eliminating or postponing the purchase of scholarly monographs in order to maintain journals collections. This option has been so widely exercised over the last two decades that the market for and publication of scholarly monographs has dramatically declined.

Providing access to the information through increased interlibrary loans and/or the use of commercial document delivery services, through resource sharing among a group of collaborative libraries, or through licensing of electronic access and transmission of information on local or wide area networks. Systems and policies are still in their infancy, as both librarians and publishers hope that collaborative studies of technology and usage, some of them already in progress, will answer the many technical and economic questions surrounding setting up new ways to price information.

Seeking additional funding from government and private sector grants, from endowments and gift funds, and from revenue generating activities, such additional funds to be used for the purchase of materials. Libraries have not to date preferred this option because increasing competition among higher education institutions for such funds means that libraries cannot count on higher levels of income from such sources.

An interesting productivity and personnel trend is that public service functions are requiring more skilled, professional staff as technical services functions shift more to support staff or are even outsourced. While two-thirds of a university library's employees may have consisted of non-professional support staff, there has traditionally been little turnover in these positions and great resistance to change. In public universities support staff are likely to be civil service and/or unionized employees. Yet, as in most industries, the lower level and less skilled jobs have been eliminated more rapidly than high skilled or professional jobs.

Allocations for automation, including capital investment in computers and other equipment, are increasing more rapidly than any other budget area. Automation costs today may represent up to twenty-five percent of the total library budget. This allocation includes services from groups such as OCLC or intra-institutional groups such as a university computer center. Finally, there is a steady five to ten percent of costs associated with administration, including staff training. Librarians have many masters. They may be accountable to university administrators, faculty, boards, donors and—in the case of public universities—legislators.

Libraries' financial accountability to university administrators or their governing boards is to stay within budget and to manage their funds reasonably and effectively. The quality of a university library's collection and services is central to the faculty's teaching and research. The faculty are a powerful constituency and at some universities decide how the library's materials budget is spent. In other institutions, librarians make purchasing decisions, but usually with significant faculty input. Reporting may occur to various governing boards of the library and the university, and to the governing boards of regional and national accrediting and standards agencies.

University libraries may be accountable to legislatures and/or private donors to ensure that money has been well spent. Donors and foundations also often have interests and expectations concerning the excellence, reputation and quality of the institution, and may require acknowledgment in the form of the naming of buildings or collections or in other forms of public recognition. Students are the largest group of other stakeholders, with marked influence on library hours, study space and service allocations. Many students, and generally the parents of students, may be more interested in the libraries' technological capabilities and collections. Alumni have expectations regarding the prestige of their university libraries and the maintenance of traditional collections, and they too look for access to library collections and new technology.

Local community taxpayers also want access and expect "more for less" in relation to the taxes they are willing to pay. Consortial colleagues expect prompt response to interlibrary loan requests and, increasingly, collaborative involvement in networked information and shared resources agreements. The professional community of librarians looks to university librarians to provide leadership in special projects, especially in preservation, new technology and cooperative resource development. Managing budgets well and educating the stakeholders to perceive libraries and their services as essential to the institution are key survival skills for library executives.

Effective public relations, communication and information on library services is part of this educational outreach. Libraries today also need to develop credibility in delivering services efficiently and to be proactive in providing new services that other institutions or departments cannot or do not provide. Librarians need to anticipate customer needs--for example, archiving of electronic materials. The benefits of electronic publishing include increased speed of publication and ease of soliciting user feedback, which can be incorporated into or tagged to appearnext to the original work.

Electronic publication provides the potential for reinventing traditional peer review by making it practical for subscribers to volunteer their services as reviewers. Even when the final product is a print publication, electronic technology for editing and production functions, e.g. capturing authors' keystrokes, editing on-line or on disk, typesetting, and producing/printing/duplicating/copying information, may ease production, require less labor and reduce costs in the production process. Similarly, electronic production requires personnel with a large amount of training in many technical fields, probably better trained and better paid than the personnel required for traditional print publishing.

Electronic information is potentially easy to change, use and publish in a wide variety of formats. It offers extraordinary opportunities for developing new kinds of searching engines, both within an original work and at the library level. Obsolescence and technological advancement are, however, issues which must be considered in evaluating the economics of electronic storage. As an alternative to physical storage, electronic storage becomes one answer to the question of where the archiving and preservation of the scholarly tradition should occur.

Another possibility is that libraries might develop collaborative contracts with publishers, by which the publishers maintain the archive of their own publications. Some characteristics of electronic publishing are more ambiguous. This ambiguity can stem from several factors: the number of potential "self-publishers" with access to networks, the interactive nature of certain electronic forms, the potentially public, i.e. networked, nature of many of the steps in the publishing process, e.g. peer review and commentary. In short, in an electronic environment, the authorship, identity and ownership of a work can become less clear because of the collaborative efforts to create it and the multiple inputs to construct it. The digital environment means that every copy is a technological equal of the original. Absent printed output, content may exist without form.

Paper becomes an interface, a volatile, disposable medium for viewing information on demand, or a storage medium. It no longer serves a primary function as a communications medium. That attribute is performed by the computer's monitor screen. The PC has made "desktop publishing" an option for any author, researcher, scientist, scholar, student or lay person. Electronic publication sometimes replaces, sometimes supplements and sometimes parallels traditional print publication. It may shorten the distance, smooth the path or offer alternate routes between researcher and end user, but it will not eliminate the need for the functions now performed by publishers and librarians which add value to the scholarly communications process.

Nonetheless, the electronic environment will change financial, technological and intellectual functions and value added activities. Hybrid publication systems require costly parallel paths of paper and electronic publishing. The majority of costs for acquisition, peer review, editing and conversion of text and illustrations into a digitized format are still required for all of the equivalent electronic methods of dissemination, and will, in fact, require redesigning work flow. It will be interesting to see if public entities and universities, which now assume much of the costs of computer networks, will be willing or able to continue to assume the costs of modernization and operation.

Therefore the need for publishers (alone or together with others) to take and manage the financial risk of publishing, and its added value to everyone in the information cycle, could increase. Publishers would argue that voluntary action on the part of academic authors to retain their own copyrights and to grant publishers one-time rights to publishing their articles has the potential to destroy the scholarly communication process because of the increased complexity and costs for negotiation of rights, and because limited licenses reduce publishers' opportunities to gain additional revenue from a particular work to help offset costs. Licensing arrangements are likely to change and expand in any case.

They are effective to the extent they define user communities for client services or marketing needs, or expand the applications and reach of scholarly works. But they can be misapplied to enhance dominant positions or restrict access to information. Some copyright clearance centers administer compulsory licenses, a controversial option in the U.S. It is generally agreed, however, that if any licensing process is overcomplicated, it will be costly and may not prevent abuses such as unauthorized use, redistribution, etc. The electronic age may create new pricing models for information, such as those being tested by the TULIP Project. Although computer technology provides a practical means for auditing as well as tracking each discrete use of information and each information user, publishers do not yet have the sufficient experience to know how to price information "by the piece." It is unclear whether selling by the article is economically feasible.

Transaction-based models may or may not allow free "browsing." Some librarians suggest eliminating bound, catalogued journals at the local level by offering information to end users on line from a central source. Others suggest-- and are implementing-- "deselection." They assert that scholars are fed up with the cost, inflexibility and inadequacy of print products. They want to distinguish "crucial" journals and decide which other sources need to be replaced, perhaps by identifying groups of scholars to create electronic alternatives to expensive journals. Still others advocate an incremental pricing model, such as that used for mass paperbacks or microfilm, where the original print format is priced to carry pre-publication costs.

The scholarly communication process need to find ways to decide what information to put on electronic networks, CD-ROMs or other systems, and how to manage, provide access to and license data use in a way that protects the producer. For example, some publishers are investigating what happens when a library licenses electronic tapes from individual publishers and makes them available through its own interfaces. Scholars will need electronic "super-catalogues" and multi-level catalogues that incorporate full-texts, standardized access points, and a bibliographic place holder. Almost every user of Internet complains about "junk overload," and as yet unmet needs to sort, organize and index new information sources.

Much electronic information seeks users, instead of users seeking information. Computer-maintained individual profiles may become important as screening mechanisms, although there are many questions about how to develop efficient but flexible profiles or software "intelligent agents." There are varieties of narrowness and broadness required for information searches, and all points on the specificity continuum must be accommodated. Generally, the technology to enable librarians to develop a new generation of information searching functions is young, but the added value of the activity can only increase in the digital environment.

Technological change is also occurring in the design of information materials. The wide-spread use of personal computers has made everyone a potential book designer. The need for, and added value of, effective visual design increases in multimedia, which is richer, contains more content, references more widely, and may involve not just illustrations but moving pictures and music or other sound. Applications of multimedia technology to scholarly and professional information have begun--for example, with the ADAM anatomy CD-ROM for medical students or medical continuing education CD-ROMs to teach surgeons new procedures. These sorts of projects require high skill levels among designers and programmers.

On the other hand, much of the information sent over the Internet has devalued the design function in order to use the universal ASCII transmission format. Users may impose their own visual designs on incoming electronic signals if a journal, for example, is available only on line or via a local area network. That should lead to a need for upgrading equipment and increasing speed on networks to facilitate design functions. Or users may need to decide to what extent they value good design. They also benefit from electronic data base technology because it reduces user error rates. Spelling and the accuracy of text references, for example, are easily checked when the entire work of an author is on CD-ROM. New photocopying technology such as DocuTech increases the ability to anthologize and adapt data for a variety of uses and users, and to print small numbers of copies economically.

These new opportunities enhance, rather than replace, traditional printed product. Few participants in the information cycle expect print information to disappear. Significant change is occurring as new information communities are created. Scholars perform peer review through use of and commentary on what is on line; the "invisible college" has evolved into new "virtual" clusters of researchers, writers and observers who transcend disciplinary and institutional changes. Librarians will bring people together with information in an integrated system of text and image data bases, and provide them with online tools to build, maintain and share databases.

Librarians are developing new collaborative roles with faculty. The interpretive, evaluative and guidance skills of library professionals will therefore continue to be highly valued in the electronic age. Electronic access to and delivery of information can create a whole new interpretation of "one stop shopping," where the one stop is a scholar's workstation, and the library is virtual rather than locative. This is at the far end of the scale of library decentralization, and has engendered discussion on some campuses about how the library or the university computer center should relate in controlling the menu, defining the structure and acting as gatekeeper of electronic information. The added value of libraries' reference and cataloging functions will become more important in a world of electronic publishing, though the form will change as libraries become partners with information management systems.

Much of the work which librarians do in the area of reference and guidance, however, will be free of the physical constraints of the library. Librarians are challenged by electronic publishing just as surely as publishers. Libraries have become the largest customer of indexing and abstracting services, not actually owning collections but using cataloging, abstracting and indexing services to permit patrons to select required materials.

Librarians add value to the scholarly communication process by preserving culture and assuring democratic access to our shared history through archiving and indexing. CD-ROMs, for example, were considered of marginal use, something of a "transitional technology," in the view of librarians. There are scenario-specific assumptions spelled out in each written description. Value-added functions had been provided by both publishers and librarians, but both groups were overcome by self-publishing and Internet distribution.

Some value-added functions are traded off in exchange for eliminating the bottlenecks around timelines and affordability. New mechanisms for delivery of information now dominate. Interfaces for end-user access such as NCSA Mosaic and its successors provide the navigating and screening processes, and users extract and input material they wish to use without formal "publication." Networks provide document production processes, archiving, and cost recovery mechanisms. Software developers produce tools for automatic cataloging, navigation/mapping/linking and usage tracking, and provide these tools free or for a fee to network operators.

Entrepreneurs who advertise their wares on the net are plentiful. These wares include offers of help in finding needed information. These are mostly the more aggressive librarian-trained individuals seeking new work. Most publications still appear in print, with a slow migration toward electronic publication by commercial publishers and a more rapid migration to the electronic form by not-for-profit publishers and self-publishers. As yet, few people are making money over the network; still, user friendly interfaces, searching tools, encryption and authentication technology are all developing rapidly. The roles of publisher and library remain similar to the present but begin to evolve into a collaborative partnership, motivated both by new technology and by the demand for change from the constituencies of both libraries and publishers.

The formerly distinct roles of library and computer center are merging as technology becomes as important as collection development. Publishers continue to identify and seek out good scholarship and assure that material is peer reviewed before publication. Publishers' methods of operation change as they begin to invest in producing their material in digital form, so that they can provide material over networks, in print, on CD-ROM, or in hand-held computer form. Authors submit work to book and journal publishers as they do now. Libraries continue their role in collection development, cataloging, storing and archiving material.

2

Online Library Management

In 1966, the first online system, IBM 1620 was located in the field of library. The equipment in the library consisted of IBM 1033 prints and 1031 card readers, which were similar in operation to the 357 Data Collection System, requiring insertion of machine-readable book cards and borrower identification badges. Although transaction information was conveyed directly to the computer as it occurred, it was stored on a separate daily transaction pack and was merged with the main circulation file only on a once-a-day batch processing basis.

The system did not include item-specific online query, so that it was still necessary to use offline batch-produced circulation lists to trace circulation information pertaining to a given item. For these purposes, the system was much like wholly offline batch processing systems. What set it apart from those, however, was its ability to perform two important functions online: checking borrower registration numbers for validity and checking each returned item against an online holds file.

Each time a borrower identification card was inserted into the designated slot of the 1031, the borrower number was automatically checked against a computer-stored file of valid borrower numbers. If the borrower's number did not have a counterpart in the file, that fact was generated immediately on the 1033 printer. This was a major improvement over completely offline operations. Where such validation, if done at all, could be performed only by manual lookup in a printed directory of borrower numbers.

Another early online circulation system was implemented in late 1967 at Midwestern University in Wichita Falls, Texas. The Midwestern system was unique in that it was, at least insofar as its designers know, the first and perhaps only online circulation system to operate on an IBM 1401 computer, a decidedly second-generation machine. Like the Illinois State Library system, Midwestern used IBM 1031 input stations and 1033 printers, validated borrower identification numbers, and checked items against an online holds file.

But it went further than the Illinois system in several important respects. Not only did the Midwestern systems check borrower numbers during a charging operation for general validation, but it also determined if a borrower had any outstanding overdue items or unpaid fines. If so, the computer generated an immediate list of the charges on the 1033 printer. The system had an online query capability, albeit restricted to searching on a borrower number.

The keying in of a number prompted the computer to respond by printing a list on the 1033 containing all items charged to that borrower. But perhaps the fundamental difference in the Midwestern system was that the main circulation file was online in the strict sense of the term, with the file being updated immediately upon completion of each transaction, rather than in a batch mode. In September 1968, the Booth Library at Eastern Illinois University in Charleston began to operate its own version of a online circulation system using a third-generation IBM 360/Model 50 computer and the IBM 1031 input stations and 1033 printers.

The Booth system had the basic functional characteristic of the Midwestern system, but with an important additional query feature. The Midwestern system had query capability by patron number; the Booth system supplemented this with item query by call number. By entering a particular two-digit code followed by a call number, a terminal operator could retrieve bibliographic information and current circulation data about a specific item. Queries of this nature were made using an IBM Cathode Ray Tube (CRT) terminal located at the circulation desk. Since the Booth Library online file was an inventory file containing an abbreviated bibliographic record for nearly even item in the library—not just items currently charged out—the scanning capability allowed shelflist searching of the entire library collection.

The structure and search capabilities of this system suggested possible extension as a public-access tool, and in fact plans were announced to locate a public-access CRT terminal near the card catalog in fall 1971. Still, the known item query capability of the Eastern Illinois system allowed more immediate information about the circulation status of an item than was possible in an offline system. In the early 1970s, a number of academic libraries began to incorporate minicomputers in their circulation operations.

A significant feature of these systems was that at least part of the processing hardware was located in the library itself, although a larger computer, outside the library, still played an integral role. Typically, the minicomputer in the library contained certain files for immediate online access and captured transaction data for later batch transmission to as larger computer located outside the library on which the main circulation file was stored. While some of the operations remained offline, this setup realized the benefits of online processing for certain critical purposes.

One of the most common minicomputers in this type of configuration was the IBM System/7 in use in circulation control in at least six libraries by early 1974. In the system operational at the University of Pennsylvania in Philadelphia, five online files were stored in the minicomputer. Each of these contained critical information against which various types of transactions were checked. There were three item files against which renewal attempts and discharges were checked. A call number file contained the call number of all items placed on hold, the access number file contained a list of all items recalled, and a reserve book file contained all items for which in request had been placed to transfer the item to a reserve book collection upon its return.

Once a day, this file was transmitted to the main computer, an IBM 370/Model 168, located at the university data processing center, for batch updating of the main circulation file. This transmission, usually involving information for about 3,000 transactions, required about 30 minutes. For the most part, improvements, gained in the Online circulation systems of the late 1960s and early 1070s over what was possible in an offline system were focused on immediate access to information about restricted items, such as holds, and better control of patron privilege.

Although improvements regarding access to information about restricted items enhanced public service by allowing more rapid reshelving of returned items and a better system for regulating holds and ensuring identification upon return, these benefits were not always immediately evident to the average library user. The second common capability, immediate access to Online delinquent patron files, could as likely cause ill feelings as goodwill between the library and its users.

The lack of reliable backup measures, inexperience in dealing with online systems, and continued reliance on batch-produced circulation lists combined to make early online circulation systems less than revolutionary in terms of public service. At least one facility, the Simon Fraser University Library, had so many problems and so much user discontent with its online system that it abandoned online and reverted to its earlier offline system." Perhaps the outstanding example during the early 1970s of online circulation system that could, in fact, facilitate user services to a degree not possible in an offline system was demonstrated by Ohio State University's Library Control System.

The entire philosophy behind the design and application of the system for the Ohio State University libraries was, as described by Hugh Atkinson, "that the system should be one which would speak to the problems of its users rather than simply the problems of the library." These problems included, among others, a decentralized library structure consisting of a main library and more than 20 branches. Only one catalog—the main library's—contained complete information for all items in all 21 libraries. Similar to several earlier online circulation systems, Ohio State opted for an "inventory" file approach in which the main machine-readable database contained records for all items in the libraries rather than an "absence" file, which would have contained records only for those items in circulation.

This principles as fundamental at Ohio State since the system was to be used as a locator file as well as for circulation operations. A massive conversion effort—perhaps the largest of its kind carried out by any library to that date—was contracted to a vendor, which put into machine-readable form records containing call number, unique item number, author, title, date of publication. Library of Congress card number, language code, from of publication code, and holding for each of 1 million distinct titles and 2.5 million items. The key to the Ohio State system was its items query capability. Searching was possible by call number, title key, and a combination author/title key.

When the desired item was retrieved, it was possible to see which library or libraries on campus owned a copy of the item, and whether each copy was charged out. Search terminals were available in the main library and in most of the branches. Thus, the entire union catalog of the libraries' holdings could be assessed from any library in the system. Although this in itself was a fundamental improvement over the single union catalog in the main library. An item not already checked out in one library could be charged on terminals located in any a copy was found to be available in a different branch library, the circulation attendant could issue a command that would generate a charge slip in the branch library that had the copy. The item would be retrieved in that library and placed on a shelf to await later pickup by the patron.

The online union catalog, showing location and circulation status of each item throughout the system, combined with the capability of remote charging to remove much of the patron uncertainty that was inherent under prior circumstances. The Ohio State University library system, like all other online system, was not entirely free of problems, but many of them could eventually be alleviated by design changes and the system was such an improvement over earlier conditions that the problems were of comparatively minor consequence. The impact of this system on library service was probably best exemplified by the fact that, during the first 18 months it was in operation, circulation at the Ohio State University libraries increased by more than 40 percent.

The system was an important achievement owing to its scale of implementation, its query capabilities, and its emphasis on public service problem solving. The same system was later taken by Atkinson to the University of Illinois and implemented; today it is the basis of an important networking system in libraries throughout Illinois. Apart from circulation, the late 1960s and early 1970s saw the development of a number of online technical processing systems. One of the earliest acquisitions systems was designed at the Washington State University Library in Pullman and was implemented in 1968; an online serials control system was up and running at University Level in Quebec the same year. Predating both of these was the beginning of a comprehensive online library system at the Redstone Scientific Information Center in Alabama. Some parts of the system were operational as early as 1966.

And by the early 1970s, acquisitions, cataloging, authority control, serials check-in, and circulation were online.

Offline computerization had been an important development in acquisitions, providing for machine-assisted production of purchase orders, improved methods of fiscal control, and more timely updating and generation of status lists. Still, a significant amount of from handling and paper file maintenance remained in many of these systems. The online acquisitions systems developed in the late 1960s and early 1970s represented major improvements by reducing the amount of manual handling and maintenance of paper products, as well as further enhanced those functions that had been performed well in offline computerized system.

In late 1960s, the online christened LOLITA, online acquisitions system required nearly seven "staff years" in programming, systems, and clerical labor to develop. It contained three Online files: order/in-process file contained three display screens of information input when an order was placed, and updated as an item passed through the acquisitions and cataloging procedures. The first screen included basic bibliographic data, the second screen contained accounting data, and the third screen allowed for local cataloging information such as call number and location. The amount of time and file maintenance that this system saved the staff, particularly when compared with a manual system, was considerable.

One of the greatest contributions made by online systems in general was the expansion of access points, and these early acquisition systems were no exception. It was possible with an offline system to produce lists or maintain paper copies of order forms by more than one point of access, such as by order number, author, and title if desired, but that merely increased the number of lists to be consulted or files to be maintained. As a result, the number of listing parameters was usually minimized in offline systems.

In online systems, all files and their indexes could be maintained in the computer, and multiple access points to a single record would not mean an increase in hard copy materials to be consulted or maintained. LOLITA, however, only provided to access points, order number and author, to each record in the system. The early online acquisitions systems retained some of the capabilities that had been included in their offline predecessors, but the newer systems were much improved in quality, speed, and ease of handling.

LOLITA, along with several other early systems, provided for handling of partial shipments and authorization of partial invoice payments, capabilities that were handled, if at all, only with some difficult by offline systems. The fund accounting component of LOLITA was also successful. A year-end encumbrance, could be generated in 20 minutes, and LOLITA was to only much faster, nut also judged more accurate and detailed in a controlled comparison with manual ledgers. Perhaps the most important characteristic of online acquisitions systems was that, in most cases, it was only one part of a broader integrated technical processing system that brought the acquisitions and cataloging functions closer together.

The online order record, upon receipt of an item, became an online cataloging record. This greatly reduced duplication between acquisitions and cataloging and also provided an end product consisting of a machine-readable bibliographic record for each item entering the collection. In LOLITA, the final steps in the online processing after an item had been received were for a cataloger to verify the bibliographic information originally entered by the acquisitions department and the complete the record by adding local cataloging data. The completed record was removed from the online file, but not before it had been copied onto magnetic tape as a permanent machine-readable record.

An important feature in the development of online technical processing systems was the incorporation of Library of Congress MARC records. Records on MARC tapes were transferred into the local online systems in various ways. A common feature across systems was that each new order was searched against a locally maintained MARC file, and when a match occurred, the appropriate MARC record entered the local system as the source for bibliographic information for ordering and eventual cataloging. One of the most comprehensive uses of MARC records evolved in the University of Chicago Library Data Management System.

Orders could be searched against the MARC files, and there was a retrospective searching capability whereby incoming MARC records were searched against the local bibliographic file to identify previously created local records as potential candidates for bibliographic upgrading by the new matching MARC record. These features in one from or another could be found in other systems, but an interesting feature of the Chicago systems was its use of MARC tapes as a collection development tool. Subject profiles, defined by Library Congress classification numbers and ranges of numbers, could be maintained online, and each incoming MARC tape was matched against them.

The result was an offline list of items falling into each subject profile for use in identifying potential orders for the library. The system also allowed access to these lists online if a bibliographer wished. The system also allowed access to these lists online if a bibliographer wished. Supplementing the LC class number profiles were certain national bibliography online profiles used to identify potential orders from an area studies prospective. In addition to profiles designed to identify items of potential interest for the library, the University of Chicago system also included a capability designed to assist in better control over blanket orders from publishers.

The first four digits of an International Standard Book Number (ISBN), MARC field 020, are unique to each publisher. Each record on the MARC tapes was automatically searched on these first four digits at Chicago. The system could then generate lists of items published by each publisher with whom Chicago had a blanket order arrangement, and these lists could be used to assist in monitoring receipt of blanket order items. Left with an alternative of in-house, single-library development projects, only the largest and most well endowed libraries could have used an online system for any technical support systems during the 1970s.

As early as 1967, however, a second alternative was being formulated, and the outgrowth of this and similar efforts was the evolution of four system—OCLC, RLG, WLN, and UTLAS—whose use by the early 1980s, extended into several thousand libraries on the North American continent. Although some libraries continued to develop their own in-house systems for certain library functions, it was apparent by the mid- 1970s that automated cataloging in particular was evolving in a different direction. The basis of this transformation was the Ohio College Library Center (OCLC), a system based on the simple premise that, recognizing minor local variations, cataloging data for a given item were essentially similar from library to library.

The Library of Congress MARC project had been as major breakthrough in the concept of shared cataloging information in an automated environment, but the general pattern of sharing had been unidirectional and on an institution-by-institution basis. MARC tapes were sent from the Library of Congress to subscribing institutions, each of which then loaded the tapes and manipulated the data on its own computer. The idea that evolved for OCLC was a central file of cataloging records that could be maintained on a single computer system and accessed through terminals sharing dedicated communications line connected to that computer. Not only would this enable libraries to share a MARC file, but it would centralize development costs of the system and virtually eliminated the need for each participating library to use the host institution's computer system.

Because the Library of Congress cataloged only portion of the universe of materials received by libraries, and since the MARC tapes included only the OCLC online system was the capability for allowing original input of records, using the MARC format, by the participating libraries themselves. The impact of this is seen by the fact that even by the end of the decade, less than one-fourth of the master bibliographic records in the OCLC database had been supplied by the Library of Congress. OCLC was chartered in 1967 and Frederick G. Kilgour named as its executive director. System production first began with offline batch processing in 1970; 54 member academic libraries in Ohio submitted punched IBM cards with Library of Congress card numbers of items for which they wanted catalogue cards produced. The punched cards were searched against a file consisting of the Library of Congress MARC records, and when a match occurred, catalogue cards were generated and sent back to the requesting library within two weeks.

In 1971, OCLC went online, installing terminals that allowed each library to search the growing OCLC On-Line Union Catalogue (OLUC), the bibliographic database of the system. The library could order catalog cards merely depressing a couple of command keys on the keyboard attached to the CRT display terminal. During the first several years of OCLC online operation, a number of far-reaching decisions were made that would enhance-and sometimes plague—the cooperative effort. The display format revolved around the concept of a bibliographic 'master record'; in theory there was to be only one record in the database for any given bibliographic entity. When this master record for an item was retrieved by a library, any of the MARC fields could be modified to reflect local practices with respect to subject headings, forms of name entry, local call number, and so on; virtually any element in the record could be modified.

All local changes were reflected on the catalog cards printed offline at OCLC and mailed to the library. These modifications, however, were not stored permanently online for the library. Therefore, when a library retrieved a record it had previously used for cataloging, the bibliographic master record was displayed online, without the local modifications that the library had previously made. The lack of capability to permanently store local information was probably justifiable in OCLC's initial stages. The amount of storage required to maintain this data for each cataloging use of each record by each library would have been enormous, especially since most members of OCLC at that time had a low incidence of adding copies for titles they had already cataloged once.

Nevertheless, it was not long after the system went online that some members began to express concern over the lack of a permanent online record containing local modifications for previously cataloged materials. A characteristic of OCLC during the 1970s was a perpetual gap between announced plans and actual implementation, and the permanent storage and display of local cataloging data—or at least of a scaled-down version of local holdings from selected fields—perhaps provides the most exemplary illustration. The strategy initially used in creating the online file of bibliographic master records in OCLC revolved around the creation of as large a database as possible in as little time as possible.

This may be overgeneralization, but there is little doubt that it was prevalent enough so that a great many of the permanent master records entered into the database by member libraries in the early years suffered in quality and completeness of information. Master records, particularly for retrospective cataloging entered into the database, were frequently created from a description taken solely from the shelflist card of the first member library to convert the title. Thus quality and completeness depended in great part on any given library's past shelflisting practices, on the library's policy for input of new records into the database, and, beyond that, on the accuracy of the terminal operator.

The philosophy of rapid creation of a database at the expense of detail and completeness of record could be seen in OCLC's approach in 1975 to providing records for serials titles, for which a specifically designed MARC format had only recently become available. To greatly increase the number of serials records in a short time, tapes of the Minnesota Union List of Serials (MULS) were loaded into the OCLC database. Although MULS contained accurate information as far as it went, it was primarily a locational tool and provided very abbreviated bibliographic data for cataloguing purposes. Perhaps the greatest quality control complication in the long run was the extreme difficulty of upgrading master records when a mistake was detected or information found to be incomplete.

Written forms had to be completed by a member library and mailed to OCLC; when received, the master record was examined by OCLC staff and modified according to the reported additions or changes. This process was time-consuming and cumbersome for member libraries, and not exactly a foremost staffing priority at OCLC. The result was that a library could easily retrieve a master record containing an obvious typographical error that presumably had been modified locally by any number of other libraries for their own card production, but that remained in the master record due to backlogs at OCLC in record upgrading.

Owing to the prominent role of the OCLC database in the Conversion of Serials (CONSER) project, a limited number of libraries were given the capability of making permanent online modifications to OCLC serials master records from their own terminals, thus bypassing the manual error reporting procedure. This proved a tremendous success. The possibility of enabling a small number of libraries a similar online capability for records in other formats was a topic of discussion for several years, and was finally initiated in mid-1984. The approach used in creating its database and the difficulty in correcting errors in master records earned OCLC a reputation in some quarters as a 'dirty database.' To be certain, many early records in the database did suffer from lack of quality control.

An often overlooked factor by critics, however, was that OCLC was an experiment without direct precedent and included among its membership a segment of the library community that had virtually no previous experience with any type of library automation. OCLC was not the first online system used for collective representation of cataloging data fro a number of independent libraries, but immediate predecessors were based on centralized input and thus centralized control. This was quite different from the structure of OCLC, in which any member library could input an original bibliographic master record for an item. Given this degree of autonomy and decentralization, combined with the lack of previous experience with library automation on the part of most of its members, and a lack of precedence to gauge the implications of shared databases, the early 1970s were an individual and cooperative learning experience for OCLC members which served to demonstrate both the strong points and the problem areas of cooperative ventures in library automation.

During 1972, membership was extended to Ohio nonacademic libraries, and in 1973 to libraries outside the state. Although the major computer facilities were to remain centralized at OCLC headquarters, a decentralized approach to the provision of general support services emerged by the mid-1970s. OCLC and various independent state and regional agencies entered into contracts for the brokering of OCLC services and for provision of training and ongoing assistance.

Some of these networks had predated OCLC; others were formed in direct response to the need for an agency to provide OCLC services in a particular area. Two exceptions to the general pattern of independent brokering were the formation of OCLC Western, consisting of several branch offices on the Pacific Coast, and OCLC Europe, both being service agencies under the direct administration of OCLC.

The independent affiliate networks, which have usually numbered about 20, have remained administratively separate from OCLC a relationship that has at times worked to the benefit of OCLC and at other times served as a source of conflict. Within four years after OCLC's decision in 1973 to expand its base of participation beyond Ohio, the number of libraries using the system had increased to more than 800. Increasing numbers of public and special libraries were joining, but the majority of new members continued to be academic libraries. These included many members of the Association of Research Libraries as well as medium-sized university libraries, but an influx of new participants continued from among the ranks of four-year colleges, a pattern that underscored OCLCs role in introducing automation into smaller institutions.

The concept of resource sharing was the basis for the formation of a number of formal cooperative ventures during the 1970s. One such, begun in 1974, was the Research Libraries Group (RLG), comprised of Harvard, Yale, Columbia, and the New York Public Library. Its board goals focused on the sharing of resources, collection development, and preservation and conservation of library materials. RLG felt that a common automated bibliographic system would enhance cooperative efforts among member libraries. By early

1978, the four systems under final consideration for adoption included OCLC, Standford's BALLOTS, the University of Chicago Library Data Management System, and the New York Public Library bibliographic control system. In spring 1978, RLG announced agreement with Stanford for the use of BALLOTS as the group's automated bibliographic component. Although RLG may merely have chosen what it considered to be the best available system, the choice drew strong reactions from within and outside the group. In June of the year, Harvard announced withdrawal from RLG, although Director of Libraries Douglas Bryant indicated that the choice of BALLOTS was not the motivating factor.

In comparing the online features of BALLOTS and OCLC, there is no question that BALLOTS was the far more sophisticated and flexible technical processing system. Unlike OCLC, it also provided for online storage and display of an individual library's cataloging data in a network environment, as well as other features such as searching by title keyword and subject, not available on OCLC. Although on a smaller scale than OCLC, BALLETS had also proved capable of serving as a shared system as early as 1975 when seven public libraries in California entered into a networking arrangement with Stanford, and the number of libraries using it has increased since then. The greatest source of resentment among OCLC libraries about RLG's selection of BALLOTS was probably not so much the choice itself as it was the accompanying implicit, and sometimes explicit, attitude that OCLC and its 'dirty database' were unacceptable, and that the needs of RLG members were somehow quite apart from those of the rest of the library community—including those of many prestigious research libraries that remained ardent supporters of OCLC.

Equally crucial in the reaction, OCLC had come to be recognized by then as much more than a shared cataloging database. Because of library identifier symbols attached to each bibliographic record, OCLC had grown into a tremendous tool for facilitating interlibrary lending and, to many, was the most current and reliable source of occasional information available in the United States. The selection of another system by RLG virtually cut off those libraries and their collections from this source of information and ejected a major obstacle to their participation in resource sharing on a broader scale.

To many OCLC libraries and even to those using neither system, this detachment seemed a conscious and motivated effort to minimize the role of RLG members in the broader context of American library cooperation. The reaction to RLG did little at that time or later to discourage the image of elitism. Full membership in RLG, in essence, required a library to be a member of the Association of Research Libraries (ARL), and this restricted potential membership in RLG to a pool of early 100 libraries. RLG permitted other libraries to apply for participant status, meaning a library could use and contribute cataloging data, but the feeling was that this did little to soften the image of elitism. BALLOTS, which in the RLG environment became the Research Libraries Information Network (RLIN), may have been functionally superior to OCLC as a technical processing system, but not all of its distinctions were carried over into the new network. At Stanford, the system had been, and remained, a full technical processing system, which traced an item and built on its online record from the initial point of ordering to its final point of cataloging.

Although any RLIN member library had searching access to Stanford's IPF, there was no capability for other members to build a similar file for their own institutions. Thus, one of the strongest features of the original BALLOTS, which provided the continuity for its realization a more complete technical processing system, did not exist under RLIN in its earliest manifestation for any library other than Stanford. During the 1970s, work was also being conducted at the Washington State Library on the design of an online bibliographic system. Supported by a $1.2 million start-up grant from the state legislature, the system went online in 1978, the Washington Library Network (WLN) was being used in 12 public and 9 academic libraries in the state, along with 2 libraries in Alaska. Later that year, 3 libraries in Idaho and 1 in Oregon joined WLN.

From the start, it was apparent that WLN was a well-designed and highly sophisticated system. It included retrieval of local information, subject access, and, not long thereafter, authority control. WLN took a cautious approach to building its bibliographic database. As in RLIN and OCLC, Library of Congress MARC tapes were loaded, but unlike the other two utilities, WLN established a standing policy to centrally review all records input by member libraries. In January 1979, the library press reported that the National Library of Australia had signed for membership in WLN had sold its system software to the National Library. All three of the major utilities—OCLC, RLIN, and WLN—were based on a centralized computer system linked through telecommunications lines to terminals in member libraries; none of the utilities up until that time had attempted to transfer any part of its system for use in another computer.

In 1978, it was not entirely clear to American library community what role WLN would assume in national bibliographic networking. Although WLN was focusing on regional cooperation in the Pacific Northwest, OCLC had also been a geographically limited system at one time, and BALLOTS had been implemented in a single library. It seemed possible that a third nationally competing system may have been emerging in the form of WLN. In 1979, however, the network reaffirmed its regional emphasis, adopting a policy that expansion outside the Pacific Northwest would-be restricted to sale of the WLN software in a manner similar to what had taken place with the National Library of Australia.

In the years immediately following, a number of such transactions occurred, including sales to the South-eastern Library Network (SOLINET), the University of Illinois, and the University of Missouri. Membership in the WLN network in the Pacific Northwest had increased to 60 members by 1980 and, as OCLC had done slightly more than two years before, WLN modified its government structure to reflect the expansion of its membership base beyond a single state. Although its impact in the United State has been limited, the University of Toronto library Automated System (UTLAS) was a fourth major online bibliographic networking system to have emerged on the North American continent during the 1970s. Implemented in an online networking mode during the mid-1070s, UTLAS had increased its membership to more than 200 libraries by the end of the decade. UTLAS membership was limited primarily to Canadian libraries, with some important exceptions. In 1980, the network signed its first member in the United States, the Rochester, New York, Institute of Technology. The following year, UTLAS signed a million-dollar agreement with a Japanese firm to broker

UTLAS in Japan. The system did not make concerted efforts to expand into the United States, but it is noteworthy that in 1981, in a comprehensive comparison of the four major utilities, the University of California at Berkeley ranked UTLAS first in overall technical capability.

The University did not, however, opt for UTLAS. In 1984, UTLAS opened a U.S. branch office in New York, and it will be interesting to see what impact this will have on its position in the nation. Over the years, each of the four bibliographic utilities has strived to become more than simply a shared cataloguing database. Development efforts by one or more have gone into acquisitions subsystems, serials check-in capabilities, circulation systems, interlibrary loan communications, online union lists, provision of Computer Output Microform (COM) catalogs, and terminal compatibility for searching other databases. WLN, OCLC, and RLIN made a tremendous impact on librarianship in the United States during the 1970s in terms of providing online cataloging capabilities, but their impact in circulation control, acquisitions, and serials check-in was negligible. Some libraries continued to develop their own in-house systems to handle these functions.

However, another alternative emerged, particularly in the area of online circulation, in the form of commercial vendors of automated library systems. Automation via unit-record equipment had been almost the exclusive domain of IBM. Remington Rand offered unit-record equipment comparable to IBMs, but its impact on the library market was negligible. IBM continued its domination into the early 1960s, when offline computer processing came into use in some libraries. As the decade progressed, however, computers manufactured by other firms began to appear in universities, corporations, and municipal facilities.

By the end of the decade, IBM was still the predominant name in computers for library applications, but it no linger maintained the exclusively it had once enjoyed. During its years of dominance, IBM had been responsible in devoting time and effort to assist in applying its equipment to the library environment. Libraries certainly did not receive an undue share of attention, but IBM representative were often assigned to help libraries with implementing applications, and the corporation published descriptions of and guides for use of its equipment in library applications.

According to estimates in the early 1970s, less than one-tenth of one percent of the computers in the United States were being using by libraries in the way. To make these facilities still less conductive as a market, even those with computers were inevitably using equipment purchased by host institutions for a variety of applications, the foremost usually not being those of the library. Libraries had little control in either the selection of equipment or in the decision to replace one manufacturer or model with another. As long as large-scale, multipurpose mainframes were the only available computers, libraries were essentially at the mercy of their host institutions. Although some libraries established excellent relations with their computer centers and did play a role in automation decisions, procurement was an unpredictable and uncontrollable environment for many.

The advent of minicomputers radically altered the computer field for libraries, enabling at least the large ones to perhaps purchase their own equipment and create a more predictable environment. A number of libraries did purchase their own equipment and designed applications software in-house in the 1970s, but another alternative began to emerge in that decade—the library-specific commercial vendor of automated library systems. In terms of the total computer market as viewed by larger corporations, libraries were too few to attract a great deal of attention, but the potential volume demonstrated a suitable market for smaller and specifically library-oriented commercial ventures.

One early commercial venture came from Computer Library Systems, Inc., later shortened to CL Systems. Inc., and later again simply to CLSI. The company's first automation efforts involved acquisitions systems, and one of its first installations, in 1972, was at the Cleveland Public Library, which had been using a batch processing system on IBM equipment for eight years. In a description of the CLSI system at Cleveland Public, Richard Palmer observed that, over a five-year period, the cost of the new online system was expected to be less than one-half the cost of the IBM batch processing system, had it been continued. In addition, the new system offered broader and more library-specific features. CLSI soon turned its attention toward circulation control. Its LIBS 100 system and other vendor-supplied systems introduced subsequently come to be known as "turnkey," a reference to the premise that, upon delivery and installation, virtually all that was required to make the system work was to plug it in and turn it on. Although in practice this has not always exactly proved to be the case, the idea was essentially sound and formed the basis on which these systems would become cost-effective alternatives to in-house development.

As so many libraries had learned in implementing their own online or even batch processing systems, the cost of design and development were considerable. With a mass-marketed system, such up-front development costs could be distributed among many customers and hence would be far less for each library then independent design and development. With a turnkey system, programming expertise was not required of the library staff or even at the host institution. Perhaps most importantly, the library's minicomputer could be operated and maintained within the library itself, and the software was marketed by vendors whose entire business was specifically library applications. Other vendors joined CLSI in the online circulation control market during the early and mid-1970s, nut for several years the field was fairly unstable.

Various companies entered and left the market, were purchased by other companies, and radically redesigned their systems. By 1975, five commercial vendors were offering turnkey automated circulation systems with varying degrees of online and offline capacity. Two years later, three of them had cased marketing efforts in the United States and another had been sold and its system totally redesigned. CLSI provided the only continuity in this short span of time. The year 1977 was pivotal, however, in that several new vendors of circulation control systems entered the market and would prove more stable than most of their predecessors. Among these were Data Phase, Geac, and Universal Library Systems.

Entering the 1980s, CLSI was still the leading force in the commercial market, with 177 installations and more than 300 other libraries remotely accessing computers located at one of the installation sites. The fastest growing computer was Data Phase with 50 installations, followed by Geac with 22. Gaylord, active since 1978, had 11 installations by 1981.

Although not actively marketing in the United State since about 1977, the Plessey online circulation system popular in Great Britain had 9 users in the United States and Canada. With the exception of early CLSI efforts, commercial activity in online acquisitions and serials control has lagged behind circulation control and did not really begin to make an impact until the late 1970s and early 1980s.

The primary source of commercial developments also differed between the two areas. For the most part, vendor-supplied online circulation control systems have resulted from new commercial ventures into the library marketplace. In acquisitions and serials control, in contrast, many of the earliest efforts came from long-established library vendors; book jobbers for acquisitions and subscription agents in serials control. Baker and Taylor's offline BATAB system was available to libraries since the 1960s, and by the late 1970s the system had been redesigned, enhanced, and offered online as LIBRIS. Around the same time, Brodart also announced availability of an online acquisitions system.

By the early 1980s, book jobbers had been joined by other vendors, such as Ringgold and Innovative Interfaces, in offering online acquisitions, as well as by each of the four bibliographic utilities. In addition, several vendors of circulation systems were in the process of testing acquisitions modules, promising even more competition. Commercially available online serials control systems have appeared comparatively recently. Two major subscription agencies, Ebsco and Faxon, each announced plans for an online system in 1981, capable not simply of ordering, but encompassing functions such as check-in and claiming, and not limited to titles ordered through the respective agency. Ebsco eventually abandoned development of its own online check-in component, while Faxon did incorporate one into its online system.

Also in 1981, the MetaMicro Corporation of San Antonio, Texas, announced a serials control software package for minicomputer application, although active marketing of this system eventually ceased. Activity in the not-for-profit sector also showed signs of life in the early 1980s, exemplified by marketing of the CHECKMATE serials control system by the California Library Authority for Systems and Services (CLASS) and by OCLC planning efforts to make its rather dormant serials check-in subsystem more attractive. Changes in the OCLC sub-system were made in 1983, but had a negligible impact in attracting new users. An interesting activity occurred with CHECKMATE, as Ebsco began to market that system when it abandoned development of its own online check-in module.

Although the bibliographic utilities emerges during the 1970s as the clearly predominant supplier of automated cataloguing systems, there were a few commercial attempts to penetrate the cataloging market. One of these was the BIBNET system, announced by Information Dynamics Corporation in 1974. BIBNET was to operate similarly to OCLC in a number of ways: it was principally intended to be a shared cataloging database; it was to contain member input master records as well as LC MARC records; the master database was to be stored on centralized computers; and library identifier symbols were to be affixed to each bibliographic record as an aid to interlibrary loan.

Several features of BIBNET were planned conspicuously different from OCLC and attempted to answer some of

OCLCs more pressing problem areas. Keyword-in-title search capability was to be available, along with plans for the eventual introduction of subject searching of the database. BIBNET users would be encouraged to access the system though a minicomputer housed in the library to facilitate local production of offline products and to reduce telecommunications cost. By using a minicomputer, libraries could retrieve records from the master database, copy them onto a cassette tape, and then break the telecommunications link. Master records copied onto the cassette would then be displayed on a CRT terminal connected to the minicomputer, modifications made to the records, and the revised records copied into a second cassette.

Catalog cards and other offline products could be printed locally, based on the modified records on the second cassette. Although access to BIBNET could be gained through means other than a minicomputer, the front-end interface was strongly promoted as the most useful for allowing flexibility. Information Dynamics had ambitious intentions for BIBNET. Not only was it to contain post-1968 LC MARC records, but there was a plan to centrally input access points into the online system for more than 3.5 million Library of Congress manual cataloging records created between 1953 and 1968. When a library retrieved such an index entry, it could notify Information Dynamics through the system that it would like a full record in the database for that title.

Information Dynamics would then create a record in MARC format for the title requested and load it into BIBNET within four days. BIBNET'S entry into the marketplace coincided with the rapid and successful expansion of OCLC. The system simply never established a firm position. A more successful venture was launched several years later by Informatics, Inc., with the introduction of MINIMARC. It was minicomputer-based, but with no pretense as a networking system. The entire LC MARC database was supplied on floppy diskettes. The library retrieved these records locally on its minicomputer and modified them according to need. For titles not found on the LC MARC database, the library could create and input records into its own working file. Catalog cards and other offline products could be locally produced.

Since a premise of MINIMARC was local processing, the system did not incur the telecommunications charges as did use of a bibliographic utility, and the overall cost were not as per-unit-dependent. On the other hand the initial investment could be as tenfold that of joining a bibliographic utility, and monthly maintenance and other costs were substantial enough to make participation in a utility more economical for smaller libraries. A limiting feature of MINIMARC was that, as a nonnetworking system, its core database was restricted to LC MARC records and was therefore smaller than those of the bibliographic utilities. Since its emphasis was so much on being a local system, it did not serve in any capacity as an interlibrary loan locational tool. In 1981, however, Informatics, RLG, and the California Library Authority for Systems and Services (CLASS) announced availability of an interface whereby MINIMARC users would be able to search the RLIN database through their MINIMARC system equipment, an arrangement that would enhance MINIMARC as a local system with access to a broader utility.

By 1981, more than 30 libraries had installed MINIMARC, and the number had increased steadily since then. Another successful commercial venture into automated cataloging was the Carrollton Press REMARC project. In 1980, Carrollton announced a five-year project in which it would convert more than 5 million Library of Congress cataloging records, not included on MARC, to machine-readable from. Libraries could submit brief data to Carrollton, in either machine-readable or nonmachine-readable form, to match against both the LC MARC database and the REMARC database being created by Carrollton. For items for which a record could be found, Carrollton would supply machine-readable bibliographic records containing relatively complete LC cataloguing data.

MINIMARC and REMARC as alternatives to the bibliographic utilities, a number of commercial book jobbers and COM vendors were maintaining machine-readable cataloguing databases for their customers. These were really a quite different matter, since initially with these stored databases, a customer did not have direct online access to its own database. This circumstance has been changing, as some of these vendors now provide online access.

Online Cataloguing

Computer-produced book and Computer Output Microform (COM) catalogues was a significant step in the evolution of the library catalog, but almost exclusively in terms of production and maintenance. Computer-produced, offline catalogues addressed many of the problems inherent in card catalogue production and maintenance, and many labor-intensive tasks that were fundamental to card catalogues were eliminated with the use of computers and machine-readable records. With offline computerized catalogues, only one unit entry record had to be created for each item; the computer expanded this record into as many individual catalogue entries as necessary and performed all alphabetization and filing tasks to maintain the catalog.

It was also much easier, at least in theory, to change a major catalogue heading; the change could be made once and applied to all effected entries by the computer-quite a difference from manually typing a new heading onto each which a change applied. However, as far ass the library user was concerned, the benefits of computer-generated offline catalogues were far less pronounced. The actual format of the catalogue certainly changed in some instances, but the basis content, and the basis avenues through which records in the catalogue could be found, rally did not. The principles used for access to entries in computer-generated book and COM catalogues mirrored those of the card catalog, and the information was often identical and sometimes even less in amount.

From the users standpoint, computer-produced book catalogues were little more than card catalogues in bound volumes, and COM catalogues little more than card catalogues in a box. Given such frustrations as dealing with multiple parts of a catalogue issues in editions and supplements, and equipment breakdowns with COM catalogues, more advantages of computer-produced offline catalogues were not noticeable to the user and, at any rate, could often be overshadowed by the logistical difficulties in using them. In contrast, many OPACs, represent a radical departure both from card catalogues and from offline computerized catalogues in their implications for the user.

Access to records can be enormously broadened in an online catalogue over what had typically been provided in other forms, but these benefits are accompanied by a new set of requirements and demands on the catalogue user. The relationship between user and online catalogue is fundamentally different from that in use of other catalogue forms. The online catalogue is interactive, not passive, and requires the user to engage in a dialogue quite uncharacteristic of card, book and COM catalogues. Just to look into the catalogue requires new procedures on the part of the user. A search must be physically, not just mentally, initiated by typing onto a keyboard issuing a command through some other means. The system will respond according to the very specific action initiated by the user.

In many instances, the user will then have to initiate further action based on the system's response, and so on back and forth until the user arrives at the desired end of the search or otherwise terminates the dialogue. This interaction and the nature of system responses represent a significant departure for the user from simply thumbing through catalogue cards or pressing a button, turning a knob, or sliding a handle on a microfilm or microfiche reader. The fact that a online public-access catalogues (OPACs) is intended for users of library materials in perhaps the fundamental distinction between this application of automation and those which serve strictly internal processing functions. Such matters as simplicity of operation or sophistication of retrieval capabilities should be important considerations in the design and selection of any automated system regardless of application, but self-evidence in operation may be less important in a technical processing system in which the library is able to exercise a certain degree of control over the selection, training, and monitoring of system users.

The design of an online catalogue must take into account a quite different set of circumstances. Considerable diversity exists among users in their level of knowledge about library catalogues and in the extent to which they are familiar with the use of computerized systems. The library will usually have little or opportunity to balance its diversity though a planned program of controlled instruction and monitoring. Most people will not use the OPAC as part of everyday routine, and hence their knowledge and skills will not be constantly reinforced.An example of the well-placed emphasis in discussions of OPACs on users and their interaction with the catalogue is the series of studies sponsored by the Council on Library Resources (CLR) during the early 1980s, aimed at gaining a better understanding of what users want and need in online catalogues, their likes and dislikes, and the dynamics of their interaction with catalogues.

Despite the vast array of differences among existing OPACs and lack of specific guidelines for development, at the base of these differences is a common goal: to design online catalogues that will allow the user maximum flexibility and yet will be easy to use. Investigations like those sponsored by CLR should help to establish a stronger foundation for realizing such a goal. Phrases such as "user friendly" have become almost meaningless because of their sometimes indiscriminate use to describe systems or features that commonsense observation show are 'anything but.' Yet the overuse, and ever misuse, of well-worn phrases does not negate the relevance of the concepts they represent. The degree to which OPACs are willingly accepted by library users will indeed depend in large part on just how user friendly these systems are.

Technical processing systems can be evaluated largely in terms of functional capabilities, or what a system can do. But the circumstances in which OPACs are still used are too different for such a simple evaluation. Equally and perhaps more important is the question of how easily system functions can be learned, understood and applied to the fullest extent by a diverse group of users. For any given characteristics in their operation, OPACs are still simply too new, and their use still too little understood, to be able to state categorically that one approach is somehow "better" than the other.

Fundamental to all of the features described is the most basic improvement that OPACs have made on other forms of the library catalog: the expansion of avenues of access to catalogue records. Although the purposes of the library catalogue are not case in stone and depend on one's perspective, one set of standards by which library catalogue functions have been measured throughout the twentieth century is the principles of Charles Ammi Cutter as noted in his Rules for a Dictionary Catalogue. Cutter enumerated three major "objects" of a library catalogue.

A catalogue should allow someone to find book if its author, title, or topic is known. A catalogue should fulfill a gathering function, showing what a library owns by a given author, on a given subject or in a given type of literature. A catalogue should provide assistance in the change of a book, either as to its edition or its literary or topical character. A fourth commonly recognized catalogue function, although not explicitly noted by Cutter, is collection, having to do with the arrangement and relationship of headings within the catalog. Underlying most of these functions is the fundamental matter of access top bibliographic records in the catalog: the points of entry through which a record for an item may be found. Cutter's first object—the finding function—is the essential basis for access, nut the gathering and collocation functions also have to do with accessibility to records. The function least directly related to access is assistance in the choice of material, which has more to do with content of a bibliographic record than access to it. Whether Cutter's objects still provide the most viable criteria for defining the purposes of a library catalogue in an online era is debatable, and some have questioned the degree of completeness to which these objects have ever actually been realized in libraries. Cutter's principles stem from a time quite different from the 1980s.

New factors—including but not limited to those of a technological nature—should not be disregarded in defining the purposes of a library catalog. Nevertheless, Cutter's principles serve as a point of departure in many decisions of online catalogues, and concerning access to bibliographic records they still provide a convenient framework for comparing online catalogues with one another and with other forms of the library catalog. Access to bibliographic records in library catalogues has traditionally been marked by a high degree of rigidity, requiring considerable knowledge and exactitude on the part of the user.

Generally, access is gained through four types of bibliographic elements: author, title, series, and subject. Multiple author and subject headings are assigned to an item as rules or judgment dictates, but the number is usually kept to a minimum. The terminology selected for headings is also tightly controlled, with the library usually trying to establish a one-to-one correspondence between headings and the persons, corporate bodies, or concepts they represent. These practices may be understandable from a practical point of view, but they do impose certain limits on accessibility to records. The user can indeed locate an item in the collection for which the author, title, or subject is known, but only under some rather inflexible conditions. To find a record under the title, the user must know the full and exact wording of the title—not some or most of the words, but all of the words, and in their correct order.

For access by author, because of the pre-AACR practice of establishing full and singularly valid forms of names, it has not always been enough to know the from of an author's name as it appears on publications or by which the person is popularly known. It has been necessary for the user somehow to know the exact from of a person's or corporation's name as it has been established by the library, often on the basis of considerable research. Where there are discrepancies in name form, it has been up to the user to figure out the form selected by the library. Access by subject is even more problematic.

Singularly valid forms of headings are selected from among all possible equivalents, but because of the greater conceptual complexity involved, there is even greater likelihood in subject searching that discrepancies will arise between the terminology selected by the library and the vocabulary chosen by the user. The problem is further compounded by the general conservatism in libraries toward changing the vocabulary used in headings and by complicated subject heading formation and filling sequences. Such practices, which result in a lack of flexibility, are all but dictated by necessity in card catalogues; however, they were also carried over generally intact to offline versions of computerized catalogues as well. Given the capabilities of computers and the elimination of the need for manual filing, there is no strictly technological reason for some of these practices to have been retained so uniformly.

Additional access points, such as by keywords appearing anywhere in titles or assigned subject headings, could have been provided with little or no appreciable increase in human labor. Similarly, duplicate listings under variant forms of names could have been supplied in the catalogue. These expansions would have required greater sophistication in indexing and would have resulted in a far greater number of entries, and thus larger catalogues, but whether for economic reasons, ties to tradition, or something else, expansions of this type were never characteristic of offline computerized catalogues. Only with the introduction of online catalogues have such expansions taken firm hold, and they are changing the very concept of access to records in the library catalogue.

Some OPACs adhere quite closely to other forms of the catalogue in the ways in which access to records may be gained, requiring just as much exactitude and exhibiting just as little flexibility. These are essentially electronic card catalogues. Other OPACs significantly broaden, and even fundamentally change, the traditional concept of access. One technique that many OPACs use to allow greater flexibility of access to records in the catalogue is keyword, or term, searching. This feature enables a user to retrieve records on the basis of single terms or combinations of terms appearing anywhere within specified fields of a bibliographic record, such as author, title or subject heading. In finding an item by title, for example, a user can retrieve a record simply by entering one or more words in the title, regardless of sequence or position.

A number of OPACs also allow keyword searching on author fields and on fields containing assigned subject headings, and some permit retrieval on the basis of terms appearing within a variety of other bibliographic fields. Keyword searching has certain advantages over the exact order full-phrase searching required in other forms of the library catalogue. In corporate author searches, the keyword capability means that the user does not have to know the exact hierarchy and order in which a corporate author name appears in the records. For title searches, the user does not have to know the full and exact wording of the title to be able to find it in the catalogue.

A key work search capability expands, and actually alters, the traditional concept of locating an item for which, in Cutter's terms, "the author or title is known." In searches for single title or single names, although the entry of selected keyword is certainly less precise than a full title or authors, name and can rest in retrieving extraneous records. among those retrieved will be the desired items. Keyword capabilities are particularly useful in subject searching. When a catalogue permits retrieval of terms appearing anywhere within assigned subject headings, the user does not have to know the full and precise working and filing sequences of assigned subject headings and subdivisions as they appear in the records themselves. Many OPACs allow a broadened view of the subject elements in a bibliographic record; for instance, by allowing keyword searching on title fields.

Given the usually high level of correlation between the subject content of works and the terms appearing in their titles, a keyword title search composed of one or two terms can be a viable from of subject searching in online catalogues. Some OPACs, in fact, automatically retrieve from title fields when subject searches are initiated. When the user carries out a subject search, records are retrieved for items in which the search terms appear either in assigned subject headings or in the title field of a record. Whether or not this combination is provided automatically by the system, the ability to search assigned subject headings by keyword, supplemented with term searching on other fields of the bibliographic record, makes subject access generally far more expensive in and OPAC than in other forms of the library catalogue.

Some OPACs allow a use to truncate, or abbreviate, search terms. For example, many online catalogues allow retrieval of records with an author's surname and first initial. Even though the full forename may be stored on the bibliographic records, the use of an initial is sufficient for retrieval. In addition to truncation or even omission of forenames and middle names, some OPACs permit retrieval on truncated forms of surnames. Others allow truncation of keywords in titles and assigned subject headings. Entry of the term "prehist" in a title search, for example, will retrieve records containing the terms "prehist" in a title search, for example, will retrieve records containing the terms "prehistoric," "prehistory," or any other derivative in the title.

This facility often applies to phrase as well, especially in the case of searching on assigned subject heading fields. In a search on assigned subject headings, truncation on most

OPACs requires an explicit expression by the user. A special character must be keyed to indicated that a term or phrase is being entered in truncated rather than in complete form. Some OPACs require the user to supply a special truncation designator; others provide an implicit form of truncation whereby the system automatically truncates a search term or phrase for retrieval according to an internally prescribed number of characters or words, regardless of how many the user has entered. Most OPACs allow the user to combine two or more search terms through the use of Boolean operators, such as "and," "or," and "not." In most OPACs, a Boolean "and" is assumed when two or more terms are entered in a search statement, especially if the search is conducted of a single field or type of information such as author, title, or subject. Only records containing all specified search terms will be returned.

In the earlier example of entering the terms "Soviet," "East," and "Peoples" in a title search, one records for works containing all three works in the title would be retrieved. Some OPACs allow the combination of terms from different fields or serving different functions, such as an author's surname and a title word, in which case the user is generally required to enter a economic code preceding each term indicating the field or function to which it applies and then linking the terms with an explicitly stated "and." OPACs with fuller Boolean capabilities allow the user to construct search statements with other operators as well as the most common being "or" and "not." Depending on which operator is used, the result of Boolean search capabilities is to allow a user to other broaden or narrow the set of records retrieved.

Capabilities such as keyword searching expand access to records through traditional avenues like author, title, and subject. Some OPACs index other fields of bibliographic description as well. In a few OPACs, virtually every tern in every field of a bibliographic record are replaced by an all-encompassing concept of access by "bibliographic description" the more specific elements of author, title, and subject headings become simply qualifiers for refining the scope of a search. OPACs generally have not taken quite this broad an approach, although some have indexed certain additional elements, such as names of publishers, for retrieval on tern searches that act upon several different fields simultaneously.

A number of OPACs offer a more restricted idea of nontraditional access points in the from of bibliographic qualifiers that the user can employ to limit the results of a search. The two most common are language and data of publication. By including a language code or publication data or range of dates in a specified manner as part of a search statement, a user can block the retrieval of records for items that would otherwise qualify but are considered too old or too new to be useful or are in languages that the user does not read.

Other bibliographic elements could be incorporated into OPACs for purposes of qualifying search statements. The possibilities depend largely on the types of information discretely identified and consistently entered into records in the bibliographic database. For libraries with records in the MARC format, one likely source of qualifiers is from the elements constituting the fixed fields. Based on these elements, an OPAC could provide the ability to limit retrieval according to government publication, conference publication, fiction, juvenile literature, and a host of other categories.

Few existing OPACs, however, currently offer a range of qualifiers beyond the elements of language ad data of publication. In a somewhat different but not unrelated category, OPACs have attempted to address traditional limitations of access in library catalogues in the treatment of alternative forms of name headings and subject terminology. The most frequent method used by card and offline catalogues has been to provide cross-references guiding the user from variants in the form of a name or subject term to the authorized, library-established, heading under which full bibliographic entries are listed.

This technique is not altogether service-effective, since cross-reference cards can be "buried" within long lists of entries or complex headings. Online catalogues generally fall into two categories in attempting to deal with likely alternatives in the terminology through which users might seek access. One technique essentially mirrors the approach commonly used in card catalogues, namely, by cross-references guiding the user to the authorized terminology. When an online cross-reference is displayed in response to a search, the user must then key in or otherwise instruct the system to search under the authorised term or phrase.

Although this approach is similar to that used in most other forms of the library catalog, the presentation is usually more distinctive because the cross-reference message will be displayed prominently on a single screen instead of being buried among other information. Other OPACs have taken a different approach with respect to cross-references by essentially dispensing with them from the user's point of view, using instead a recognition of equivalent terms as valid for retrieval. If the library has assigned "Women" and "Females" as equivalent subject terms in an online authority file, for example, the user will retrieve the same full listing of records in a search on assigned subject headings regardless of which of these two terms is entered in the search statement.

This approach still requires the creation and use of an authority file, but the linking of terms is strictly internal and visible to the user. Other features, such as the use of word proximity in term searching, have been incorporated into some OPACs father expand the accessibility to records in the catalog, but those described here are the most common, and they significantly broaden the ways in which library users can approach catalog. Now of these features is new to online information retrieval systems used in the library environment in general; they have been standard in such systems as DIALOG and BRS for many years. What is new is their incorporation into the public catalogue librarians have long assumed that systems such as DIALOG and BRS require special expertise and training for effective use.

What is most challenging about OPACs is that at least some of these same sophisticated features are intended for people without formal training and with only limited need to use them. Taking these factors into account is perhaps the most crucial element in the successful design of online public-access catalogues and their implementation in the library environment. Because they are interactive and can offer far broader approaches to access, OPACs are a fundamentally different from of catalogue than their predecessors. The overall difference can result in greater value for the library user, but not without costs in human terms.

Interaction with computerized systems and the use of such techniques as keyword searching, truncation, Boolean combinations, and so on, involve skills that many users do not have, especially within the context of application in a library catalog. For many, lack of familiarity with computers and retrieval techniques extends well beyond use in an Online library catalog. There are still many library users for whom interaction with a compute for any purpose remains an alien experience.

This situation is changing rapidly as more and more of the population become educated in computer use, but for some time to come, unfamiliarity is a condition that must be taken into account in the design of online catalogues. With an OPAC as both a system and a catalog, the rules governing behavior can be fairly mechanically and consistently structured, even if at times they are complex.

As an online computerized system, an OPAC incorporates certain rules that dictate how a user must enter commands and how the system will react to them. In the library catalogue function, certain aspects of interaction will be governed primarily by rules and conventions adopted by the library regarding descriptive cataloging, summation of subject content, and so on. Rather than distinguishing between on OPAC as a library catalogue and as the mechanical means of conveyance, some discussions blend the two functions together.

However, it is important to recognize such a distinction on at least a conceptual level, for each purpose has characteristics that can independently contribute to success or failure in using an OPAC. Some patrons may be well versed in the use of computerized systems and their retrieval techniques, but may be almost totally unfamiliar with the library's cataloguing and other bibliographic practices that do.

in fact, influence the degree of success in using the system. Other patrons may have a fairly comprehensive understanding of the structure and organization of library catalogues, even in online form, but may be unskilled in the mechanics of using computerized systems and unfamiliar with retrieval techniques.

Any advantages gained by introducing clarity, case of use, and greater flexibility at one of these levels can be offset by undue complexity or lack of clarity at the other. By taking advantage of the power of the computer, an OPAC can be more flexible than conventional catalogue forms, but it must be so in a way that allows these new methods to be easily learned and understood. Although the rules that govern the behavior of an OPAC as a system and as a catalogue can be fairly mechanical and consistent, the rules that govern the behavior of the library user are not.

Human factors that influence online catalogue use, such as levels of knowledge, skill, and motivation, vary widely from one user to another, and even within the same user at different times. Complicating matters is the user's perception of how an OPAC works. It is one thing to say that an online system performs a certain way or that certain rules govern the structure and organization of a library catalog, but the more important consideration is the user's own perception about how the system works or how the catalogue is structured and organised.

The design features of an OPAC can either facilitate or inhibit interaction between user and system. Libraries are not always able to provide the desired level of guidance and assistance when making as significant a change as introducing a sophisticated online public-access catalog. Therefore, an

OPAC must be designed to minimize the need for offline guidance, taking on some of the instructional responsibilities and burden of assistance itself. An OPAC must be easy to use and its features easy to learn, and it must be a free as possible from retype language, confusing conventions, and complex rules that are meaningful only to the system.

The term "user friendly" may be ambiguous and trite. but the concepts it represents are perhaps the most crucial criteria for evaluating systems designed to handle the interaction between a computer, a library catalogue, and a diverse group of library users. There are certain similarities from one online catalogue to another in terms of the sequence of stages in which dialogue occurs. OPACs vary in the extent to which each stage in this general sequence is explicitly necessary, especially in the earliest and latest steps—the begin-session, file-selection, and terminate-session procedures.

Many OPACs do not require the user to instruct the system that a new search session is about to begin or to explicitly select the catalogue file. Instead, the OPAC is constantly set for a bibliographic search, enabling the user to begin searching immediately on arrival at the terminal. Similarly, many OPACs do not require the user to explicitly information system when a session is completed.

The user terminates the session simply by walking away from the terminal, and the display remains on the screen until a new search statement is entered. Even when specific begin-session or end-session procedures are required or available, their execution is normally simple and straight forward. The real substance of interaction occurs between the time a user enters as search statement and the time at which he or she feels the search is completed. The end of a search may be the display of a single bibliographic record for an item, a list of abbreviated bibliographic records containing one or more of the desired items, or a response or display that leads the user to conclude that the item or items are not in the catalog. The dialogue from entry of a search statement through final resolution may require any number of user-initiated actions and system responses.

In terms of the general nature of the user interface, it is important here to moment on two of the stages in particular. The first involves entry of a valid search statement and the initial system retrieval of appropriate records. In some OPACs, this stage consists of a single step by the user and a single response by the system. In other, there are two or more interactive steps involved. For example, the use may first be required to indicate the type of search being conducted—author, title, subject, whatever—to which the system responds by acknowledging the type and issuing instructions to enter search terms. The user then keys in the appropriate term or terms, and the system responds by providing first-level retrieval of all records in the database matching the two-step search statement.

Some OPACs, depending on the complexity of the search statement, require even more that two interactive steps before the statement is complete and records are retrieved. The second major stage of interaction involves the manipulation and refinement of the search results provided by the system at the first level of retrieval. If the search is satisfied at the first level, this will be unnecessary. In many cases, however, the search is not satisfied at first stage, and final resolution may require several steps in manipulating and refining the initial results.

Methods for Effective Online Management

Software methods and tools are effetive to manage document in digital libraries. If the documents are edited directly in the publication area, readers are exposed to every editing error and inconsistency of the document collection. The consequences of this may be small in personally published documents. However, the errors and inconsistencies that this exposes in corporate and project documents are unacceptable. Documenting the process is the first step in ensuring repeatable quality.

Digital libraries must be able to manage the history of documents over time, not just offer to readers the latest versions. For example, in a digital library that captures the history of an engineering project, there are documents that keep a record of design decisions made. The documents recording decisions usually reference other technical reports in the library as justification for the decision. An example is the selection of a hardware component to be used in a system. The organizational schemes used in corporate digital libraries are mostly ad hoc, usually influenced by business organization and project breakdowns.

Business organizations and projects are notoriously fluid. The distributed nature of digital libraries and the variety of storage solutions that networks enable have practical advantages. However, the physical protection of the documents that compose the corporate knowledge base is not one of them. Too often, knowledge captured in electronic documents is put at risk or lost because of media reuse or obsolescence. On the World Wide Web, not all electronic collections are well maintained-the degree of management of electronic collections varies considerably.

Moreover, the characteristics of the Web raise many challenges for the maintainer. Collections on the Web can be extremely distributed-not only the location of the documents is distributed, but ownership is also distributed. At the moment, the Web is less like a library and more like a huge bookshelf, containing millions of documents and links to documents. This mega shelf is subject to the activities of an army of people that keep acting upon it in ways such as adding, removing, indexing, cataloguing, rearranging, modifying, and copying documents.

Additionally, all these activities tend to occur with little or no coordination, worsening the situation. Better coordination, social protocols, and institutionalized management of collection can alleviate the situation in some cases, particularly when the owner of the collection and the owners of the documents agree to coordinate their activities.

The emerging digital topical libraries, while homed on the Web, are better maintained than the Web as a whole. They present a more cohesive and organized structure in order to support their patrons. Different automatic mechanisms have been devised in order to help manage the documents. Indexing and cataloguing are considerably easier to perform than in the pre-electronic days. Nevertheless, considerable human effort is still required to monitor the changes in documents and collections. In addition to the digital library that is provided by the "owner" of the documents there are a growing number of specialized libraries with distributed ownership. Digital documents are typically very fluid, i.e., changes are a common occurrence. Although detecting changes is easily automated, assessing the relevance of changes is not.

Typically humans are needed when facing the task of relevance assessment. In fact, "relevance" is a highly abstract, contextual, and subjective concept. Different individuals can disagree in their relevance judgment about any given change. Nevertheless, as difficult as it may be, assessing the relevance of a change is still necessary. The approach provides a way of automatically assessing the relevance of changes in the Web pages. This method is explored in the Path Manager, a system designed to infer relevance of changes to Web pages and to communicate this information to the collection's maintainer. Web readers access a rich and vast collection of information resources authored and published by a multitude of sources.

In this collection it is possible to find information on virtually every topic, varying in aspects such as point of view, validity, semantics, rhetoric, and contextual situation. In order to better exploit this collection, different systems have been developed with the goal of aiding readers by providing an interpretation or contextualization of Web pages. Before proceeding, and in order to avoid possible confusion, it is important to define the different people and components involved in the problem. Therefore meta-documents are defined as "paths" even though this is not the only possible meta-document.

Similarly, construction blocks are referred to as "Web pages" or "pages". The first group involved is the people that originally create and publish the Web pages. They are identified to as "page creators". Another group is the people that create the meta-documents or paths. This group is denoted in this document as "path authors" or just "authors". Additionally there is the group of people accessing or using the paths, which is designated as "readers".

Finally there is the group of people who has to manage the collection of paths and are referred as "administrators". It is important to consider that any given person might act in any or multiple of these roles at any given time. Pursuing approaches to assist path authors and administrators in managing continuously occurring changes in their selected collection of Web pages. While emphasis is on paths, approach will be equally applicable to other Web-based domains that need to assess the relevance of changes to Web pages authored by third parties.

A more accurate mechanism would retain cached copies of Web pages. It is easy to compare a document with a previously cached version and determine if there has been any change. In a similar way, it would be possible to check for changes within specific sections of the document. These cases would return a Boolean "yes/no" indication of change. A difficulty arises when attempting to determine the relevance of changes. The obvious approach would be to assess the magnitude or amount of change.

Unfortunately, there is not an easily computed metric that provides a direct correlation between syntactic and semantic changes in a Web page For instance, there is no clear relationship between the number of bytes changed and the relevance of the change to the reader. A large number of bytes changed might result from a page creator who restructures the spacing of a page's source encoding while maintaining the same content from a semantic and rhetorical point of view.

Similarly a small number of bytes changed might result from the insertion of a few negations in the text that causes a complete reversal in meaning. On the other hand, think of other situations where a large number of byte changes correspond to the creation of a completely different page, and situations where a few bytes are changed when the page creator simply corrects minor spelling and grammatical errors. The goal would be to efficiently obtain a measure of the semantic distance between two versions of a document.

Markup languages such as SGML and XML already specify structure rather than presentation. Even though Web pages are encoded in HTML, analyzing the changes is not an easily automated task. While HTML provides some information about the structure of the document, it is commonly used for specifying presentation rather than structure. Adding to that, page creators use HTML in extremely different ways. Paragraphs, headings and other tags are used quite diversely.

What conceptually constitutes a paragraph for one page creator might constitute several pages for another. This does not mean that HTML tags are useless for analyzing change. On the contrary, HTML tags and other features such as keywords can be used in order to infer the relevance of changes. Measuring the magnitude or relevance of changes in an automated fashion is not an easy task.

Researchers have encountered this problem in a variety of contexts and their approaches have informed work. In order to infer change relevance, it is important to classify the nature of the change. There are four categories of change that distinguish between: content or semantic, presentation, structural, and behavioral. Content changes refer to modifications of the page contents from the reader's point of view.

For example, a page created for a soccer tournament might be continuously updated as the tournament progresses. After the tournament has ended, the page might change to a presentation about the tournament results and sports injuries. Presentation changes are changes related to the document representation that do not reflect changes in the topic presented in the document. For instance, changes to HTML tags can modify the appearance of a Web page while it otherwise remains the same.

Structural changes refer to the underlying connection of the document to other documents. As an example, consider changes in the link destinations of a "Weekly Hot Links" Web page. While this page might be conceptually the same, the fact that the destination of the links have changed might be relevant, even if the text of the links has not. Structural changes are also important to detect, as they often might not be visually perceptible. Behavioral changes refer to modifications to the active components of a document.

For Web pages this includes scripts, plug-ins and applets. The consequences of these changes are harder to predict, especially since many pages hide the script code in other files. To represent the different characteristics of a Web-based document, use a set of document signatures to infer and compute similarities between two Web pages. There are some changes to Web pages that do not affect any of the previous metrics. For example, a change to an image source would not be reflected in any of the current metrics as it is not part of the text, headings, links or keywords of the document. In this case the global checksum provides a last resort to point out changes.

Combining the results of the various document signatures into an single metric of change is difficult. Some Web page changes are easily perceived while others are not. Some changes might alter the visual appearance of a page while maintaining the same structure and content. Other changes might change the links while maintaining exactly the same appearance. As already acknowledged, the relevance of change is situation dependent and no single metric will match all situations. The Path Manager interprets links in the HTML file as a list of URLs to check. In order to detect and assess the possible changes, the system retrieves all the pages from the Web, then parses their contents and creates a new signature for each page.

The page signatures obtained are compared with the previously computed signatures. Finally, based on the comparison results, the system presents users with an assessment of the relevance of the overall change of each Web page. The user can then review each page individually and if there are no relevant changes, the user can validate the current state of the pages. In order to compute the magnitude of the change, or the distance between two documents, a comparison is made between the signatures of the current version and those previously stored. The original signature is the first signature obtained. It is used to give a sense of the total amount of change since the page was selected.

The last valid signature corresponds to the last time that the user reviewed the changes and validated the pages. As time passes the user might update the valid signature as the pages change. This signature represents functional state of the page. Finally, the latest signature corresponds to the last time that the Path Manager retrieved and analyzed the pages, regardless if the user validated their state or not. Using these three signatures the Path Manager can indicate the amount of recent and long-term change for a page. The Path Manger extracts the pages from the path file and presents them to the user. Pages are identified by either their title or, when the page title is not available, their URL. Colors are used to represent the magnitude of the change.

In turn, the degree of relevance of the change is encoded by the color of the page title or URL. In particular, black means that there is no relevant change based on the algorithm chosen. Green, yellow, and red text indicate low, medium, and high degrees of changes considered relevant by the algorithm. The coloring scheme is based on user-defined trigger levels, which in turn could be used for other purposes such as not showing in the path a page that has changed more than the medium level. At this point the user might choose to validate the state of the pages by clicking on the red "Valid" button. Alternatively the user might wonder about what kinds of changes prompt the system to assess the overall relevance of the changes.

In order to support the more inquisitive user, the Path Manager can display the amount of change to the particular document signatures used in the relevance assessment. The specific change metrics are presented to the right of the page identification. In addition, the user can get more information on each Web page by selecting the page identification. This view provides the assessment of change to the page at the bottom and information about the use of the page above. For the user to be able to assess the relevance of the change, they may need to see both the content of the page and the context of its use.

The top of the detailed view for a page presents properties of the page within the path, such as the cache strategy, annotations and visibility of the page. The system will also display the page in a Web browser at the user's request. At this point the user, who might not be the same person who authored the path, might judge the page inappropriate and choose to hide the page from the viewers. While this action prevents the material from being shown to readers of the path, it does not delete the page from the path, leaving that decision to the path author.

In case there have been connection or retrieval problems, the manager can prompt the system to check this page again. In addition the user asks for metadata about the path as a whole by selecting the information button, located to the right of the path file in the main interface. Some pages are returned rather quickly, while others take longer to return. Also varying connection times means that, sometimes when a Web page seems to take too long to load, canceling the retrieval and immediately restarting the process results in the Web page being loaded faster.

Were the Web pages in a path to be checked sequentially, retrieval problems of a single page would block the retrieval of all consequent pages. Therefore the Path Manager architecture has been designed as a multi-threaded process in order to avoid possible blocks and expedite retrieval. In this scheme, each page is retrieved and analyzed in an independent thread. The user controls the maximum number of simultaneous threads. Even using independent threads, there are many possible problems when retrieving pages from the Web such as no response, slow connections, and very long pages.

The whole path checking process can also be interrupted by a general timeout or by the user clicking the stop button. Each thread evaluates one page at a time. Once it either successfully or unsuccessfully evaluates the change to that page, the thread will pick another from the set to be checked until all pages have been successfully checked or a general timeout has occurred. In order to inform and evaluate the approach and design of systems that aid in the automatic assessment of change relevance, several studies were conducted to observe how humans perceive changes of Web pages. This studies covered three kinds of change: content, structure and presentation.

In particular, content changes included modifications to the text presented, structure changes referred to modifications of URLs and the anchor text for links, and presentation changes included modifications to colors, fonts, backgrounds, spatial positioning of information, or combinations of these. Web pages were selected from paths previously created by teachers and from personal bookmarks. Each page was modified to reflect a single type of change, and was classified by the magnitude and the type of change. The experiment consisted of presenting the participant with two versions of a Web page, the original version and a possibly modified version. The person was then asked to evaluate the magnitude of change. Before the evaluation familiarized the participants with the testing software and the kinds of change.

Additionally provided a context for evaluating the changes in the Web pages by providing a scenario. The participant was asked to act the role of the Information Facilitator in a K-12 school (Kindergarten to High School). Teachers have chosen pages from the Web to teach their classes and it is the participant's responsibility to check for changes. The first task was to fill in a pre-evaluation questionnaire collecting demographic data about the participants and their computer literacy.

A limitation of the current Path Manager is that no indirection is supported. When faced with Web pages containing frames, the Path Manager does not check the pages contained in the frames. The same is true for other tags such as images or links. There is no retrieval of the pages specified in the SRC or HREF fields unless they are also included explicitly in the path. Another limitation of the Path Manager is that it does not monitor any JavaScript or other page behaviors. This is in part due to the complexity of the required parser and to the fact that this remains a moving target, where specifications and support vary constantly over time and browser type.

Finally, while the Path Manager can parse dynamically generated pages returned by CGIs, it does not recognize that they are dynamic and therefore variable by nature. Augmenting the system to recognise these, could enable separate treatment for such pages. Maintenance of distributed collections of documents remains a challenging and time-consuming task. People must monitor the documents for change and then interpret changes to the documents in the context of the collection's goals. In the context of networked library services, the necessity to integrate secondary data, catalogues and primary information has been expressed quite some time ago.

More specifically, librarians have brought to the fore the need to link abstracting databases with library catalogues; catalogues with primary information: abstracting databases with full-text primary information. These specific linking notions have evolved towards a concept of connecting all the available information, in order to come to a fully interlinked information environment. Publishers, subscription agents, researchers and libraries are all looking into ways to create added-value by linking related information entities, as such presenting the information within a broader context estimated to be relevant to the users of the information.

The omnipresence of the World Wide Web has raised users' expectations in this regard. When using a library solution, the expectations of a net-traveler are inspired by his hyperlinked Web-experiences. To such a user, it is not comprehensible that secondary sources, catalogues and primary sources, that are logically related, are not functionally linked. Links between information entities are computed in advance using batch processes and are held in a linking database. Typically, the processes use SICI-related information to detect relationships. Static links are used in initiatives like IOP's HyperCite, BioMednet's Bundled Links, Ovid's Biomedical Collection and many other commercial linking frameworks as well as in advanced electronic library services like the Los Alamos Library Without Walls and Tilburg's and Bielefeld's environments.

Static links are foolproof in the sense that following a pre-computed link will most certainly lead to the desired target. When considering solutions where bi-directional linking — from now on called interlinking — is the aim, building the linking solution requires the availability of all data that needs to be interlinked under the control of the authority creating the environment. Given the preliminary state of interoperability initiatives that might overcome this problem, the information collection must be centralized and self-supporting. Some interesting initiatives have started from a decentralized concept, where not all of the data that is required to build an interlinked information environment can be under the control of the authority creating the environment.

Therefore, the creation of a fully interlinked information environment — that would result in a true one-stop shop — would require either an information monopoly or extensive partnerships. Although some publishers call for subject-driven cross-publisher information shops with DOI as an enabling instrument, some industry observers see little tradition in the cooperation required for success. Therefore, the realization of a true one-stop shop under commercial control might not be a reachable goal. But if it is, it will most probably not come from an information monopoly that would support a static linking approach, except in narrowly defined fields.

Logical behavior by companies in the information industry would normally prevent a broad monopoly from developing. A dynamic approach seems to be more likely. In the non-commercial arena, the systems that make up hybrid library environments can be under local control, as is typically the case with OPAC and some secondary data systems. Alternatively, systems may also be under technical control of an external authority, such as a database vendor, a subscription agent, a publisher, and another library. The non-commercial parties — libraries and consortia — are in a much better position to build integrated services, since they are not copyright owners. As such, they are neutral enough to potentially receive a green light from a wide variety of information vendors, to integrate and interlink their data-collections.

Therefore, the future reality of hybrid library systems will most probably exclude linking solutions that require the local availability of all data or even important parts of it. Hence, also in hybrid library environments, linking tends toward a dynamic approach. The frameworks that have been introduced so far feed links based on the collection that the provider of the links — henceforth referred to as the authority — has within its reach, and leave no room for adaptation to the environment where the links are consumed. The linking frameworks can be called "closed."

Most environments where links are consumed are hybrid libraries, made up of OPAC systems, abstracting databases, e-journals and e-editions as well as web-services. Some of the latter can hardly be classified using traditional library jargon. In this environment, a wide range of services — that go beyond the initial aims or the possibilities of the authority — can be delivered by creatively using the available information. The combination of an information unit that a user considers to be of interest and the entire collection that is accessible in the actual environment in which he operates can lead to the provision of a wide range of extended services for that information unit. The authority can not anticipate the diversity of information that is available in the local environment.

Thus, in order to deliver links that deal with the full richness of the information environment, the authority can not just autonomously define the target(s) of a link. Rather, linking should be seen as influenced by the environment where the link will be used. It should reflect a combination of the authorities' and the consuming institutions' intentions, ultimately even the users' goals. Although these considerations apply to both commercial and non-commercial authorities, the hindrance resulting from closed linking frameworks is most significant with commercial services that follow a strategy of vertical integration that restrict the freedom to combine information from different vendors in the same environment. In a consortium environment some libraries rely on the hosting authority for all their library services, making the local environment the same as the authority's.

As such, integration can fully be dealt with by the authority. But in some consortia, participating libraries may host some information locally that is not relevant to the entire consortium, but still want it to be integrated with the whole. The mainstream of the current linking approaches excludes the involvement of the consuming institution that is required to implement such services.

The context of the environment in which the de-facto interlinked information is consumed is being ignored. Given the increasingly distributed nature of the information collection at hand, a dynamic linking approach or at least some combination of static and dynamic linking might prove to be the most realistic path leading to a fully interlinked environment. The desire to act upon information units that are being provided by an authority calls for an open linking framework that is not in place. The alternative is to create extended services using a dynamic linking approach.

Content Management

The idea of "content management" is multifaceted. One's choice of a perspective on the idea carries with it distinctive terminology, particular alliances with facets of a complex information technology infrastructure, specific limits on what content is and is not, and implied commitments to organizational and administrative priorities. Each of the three perspectives outlined below attempts to deal with various aspects of the content management issue, ranging from digital content (as objects or assets), to the people who add value to the content, to the tools one uses to add support or manage the process of adding value. For many people in the IT community, content management simply means WEB content.

The key concept in Web content management is the creation of value through a reduction in "time to web." In practice, this concept translates into more dynamic web delivery systems built on the back of a relational database tied to a template-driven workflow process that allows fewer people to create and deliver more web content. A database-driven approach to web content management opens up new possibilities within an organization to share content across units and to share in the costs of creating and maintaining digital content.

Some writers on content management have chosen to focus almost exclusively on protecting the asset value of digital objects, without regard to the purposes to which the objects may be put. From an asset management perspective, the organization of digital objects in well structured and well-documented databases is the most critical activity. The digital preservation community in libraries has tended to emphasize asset management as a key value. The present movement to specify preservation metadata requirements within the construct of the Open Archival Information System reference model is the most dramatic example of efforts define content management in terms of the archival repository.

Knowledge management

Knowledge management has traditionally suffered from the hubris of modernism: the belief that we can discover ultimate truths and organize the world according to rational principles using clever code. The idea was that we should capture and organize bits of "knowledge" in central databases. Therefore, postmodern KM can't be about management at all, because management implies external control of some definable resource. Its goal is simpler yet deeper: leveraging people.

Postmodern KM operates within and on the basis of existing behavior patterns, mining conversation streams and relationships automatically to incorporate structure and context into the information human users already manipulate. It fosters human intelligence and interaction rather than trying to replace them. This vision of content management suggests that librarians must reconcile the tensions between the structured and the dynamic, between "control zones" and empowerment, and between the Web that we access and the digital content that we provide.

These tensions are not new or particularly interesting, except in so far as they help us extend the concept of "content" to encompass a much wider range of management responsibilities for digital content than we have heretofore chosen to consider appropriate. Increasingly, libraries are being asked or expected to step up to the challenge of acquiring, organizing, and protecting digital content that they have neither created themselves (digitization) or licensed from publishers.

Examples of new generations of digital content that are just beginning to flow into and through libraries include digital products produced and distributed or otherwise published by faculty, the output of research collaboratives, graduate student theses, the electronic records or the university's administrative offices, courseware content, and streaming audio and video resources generated from courses, conferences, and other campus activities. In the Web environment, the business community has adopted the term "knowledge management" to refer to processes that use technology to leverage human expertise and know-how to create new value for the organization.

In the higher education context, knowledge management constructs are most closely tied to scholarly communication processes. Within this context, a critical issue for libraries is tension between possibly competing commitments to the process of scholarship as a discipline-based enterprise and the product of the process as an institutional imperative.

Another critical aspect of considering "content management" to be an important but limited component of the scholarly communication process is the relationship of librarians and libraries to content creators, whether those creators are faculty/authors or publishers/owners. Daniel Greenstein has recently drawn our attention to new efforts by librarians to tie the digital resources they have created or acquired more directly to academic and instructional uses of technology by scholars. "It is rare to find a digital library that is actively supporting or even integrating with academic computing initiatives, such as those that focus on the development and application of instructional learning technologies."

Today's library is "all digital" in the sense that all services and content (digital and non-digital) are mediated via web gateways. Users begin and end their scholarly work with digital information, even if there is a considerable amount of paper in between. Without some form of digital accessibility, library resources in any format are invisible and therefore unusable. Physical browsing for all but a vocal few has become a chimera. Libraries are already in the new business of digital product development by nature of their creation of digital resources, regardless of whether creation encompasses only digitization or extends to the development of specialized aggregations of digital resources.

Libraries and archives cannot possibly assume full responsibility (as they have with paper) for preserving digital information, but rather must participate in a marketplace that itself has not come to terms with the idea of lost value. Librarians are critical players in the conception of the IT marketplace but have neither exclusive claim on content management concepts or a particularly strong share of the marketplace that is driving the development of content management tools.

3

Electronic Collections

The anticircumvention provisions of the Digital Millennium Copyright Act (DMCA) were the subject of considerable controversy during the legislative debate on WIPO treaty implementation, and, as adopted, they bear the imprint of lobbying and political compromise.

Digital signatures must have a reliable way to determine that it has the right public key each time it decrypts a message or verifies a signature. For example, a digital library may insist that each article it offers be digitally signed by the author so that readers can verify the article's authenticity. This approach requires that the readers be able to trust that the library has correctly associated the authors' names with their public keys. The basic building blocks of the simplest approach to public-key infrastructure are "identity certificates" (ID certificates) and "certifying authorities" (CAs), analogous in some ways to the physical identity cards (e.g., passports) issued by authorities such as national governments. In the digital world, an ID certificate is a signed data record containing a public key and the name of its owner (and perhaps some related data items such as an expiration date).

An ID certificate is issued by a CA, which signs it with its signature key SKCA. If a user (or a service like a digital library) has a trustworthy copy of the CA's public key PKCA, it can build on its trust in PKCA to develop trust in the ID certificates (and their keys) that the CA has signed. For example, someone receives a document signed by Alice, together with an ID certificate associating Alice with her public key PKA. The recipient uses the CA's public key PKCA to verify CA's signature on the ID certificate and, if this succeeds, the recipient can then be confident in using the key in the certificate, PKA , to verify Alice's signature on the document. The user's trust in the CA consists of trust that his or her copy of PKCA has not been tampered with and trust that the CA has associated the correct public key with the name Alice.

The public-key infrastructure task also requires that there be a means of dealing with keys and certificates that have expired or been revoked. Basic security principles require that both keys and certificates have expiration dates (no password should be good forever) and that both are revocable to deal with secret keys that have been compromised. One standard version of public-key infrastructure calls for official CAs to issue ID certificates for other official CAs, thus forming "hierarchies of trust." In another approach, anyone can act as a CA (or "introducer") by signing name-key pairs in which he or she has confidence, and "webs of trust" emerge spontaneously as users decide whom to go to for introductions. More recently, the research community has developed public-key infrastructures in which certificates do more than just bind public keys to names.

Direct authorization of verification keys can be a powerful tool in Intellectual Property (IP) management and in e-business generally, enabling individual customers to do business anonymously and enabling businesses to derive much more information from digital signature verification than simply the name of the signer. The security of any encryption scheme depends on keys being difficult to guess. The analogous lesson about passwords is not widely heeded: Computer systems today are routinely broken into by "dictionary attacks," routines that simply try as a password all the words in a dictionary, along with common names, birthdays, and so on.

The more sensitive the resource to be protected, the more difficult its key must be to guess. The problem is that a good key is basically impossible for any human being to remember. As a consequence, keys are themselves stored and managed by computing systems and passed across the network; they are in turn encrypted under key-encrypting keys. A protection infrastructure becomes necessary. Because digital systems can be extremely complex, the engineering and management disciplines needed to accomplish such infrastructures have become areas for specialists. A great deal has been written about both the engineering side of system protection and about practical service operations.

Because key management can be extremely cumbersome, IP delivery middleware and the end-user applications to which IP is delivered go to great lengths to keep end users unaware of it. When a user clicks on the "play," "view," or "print" commands for an encrypted object, the appropriate decryption keys should be retrieved automatically by the application, which should then decrypt the content and present it as appropriate. The user should not have to do anything explicit to find the right key or apply it and the decryption tool. Unfortunately, the efforts to achieve such ease of use of encryption tend to work against the effectiveness of encryption in safeguarding content, at least in applications that execute in ordinary PCs. The problem can be solved to some degree by having users store their keys on removable media (e.g., smart cards), but such cards would impose significant burdens on users and distributors.

This challenge illustrates that analysis of trade-offs between ease of use and strength of protection is an important and difficult part of IP management systems development. In addition to posing some technical challenges to the developer of a product or service, the use of encryption also poses legal and political challenges. Encryption systems and products that use them are subject to U.S. government export restrictions, restrictions that are themselves subject to change, making product development and business planning difficult.

Although there are currently no restrictions on domestic use of encryption, the U.S. copyright industries clearly would not want to use one set of products and services (with strong encryption capabilities) for the domestic market and another (with weaker, exportable encryption capabilities) for the overseas market. Not only would this arrangement mean higher development and maintenance costs, it is also likely backwards: Serious commercial piracy is more of a problem outside the United States, calling for stronger encryption outside national boundaries.

The encryption export issue will thus have to be dealt with if encryption is to play a prominent role in IP management. Like public-key cryptosystems, digital signature schemes are currently cumbersome to use because of the lack of infrastructure for managing public keys. There is good reason to believe that an appropriate infrastructure will emerge soon, however, because of the enabling role that digital signatures could play in electronic commerce.

Unlike encryption, digital signature technology is not encumbered by export restrictions. The freely exportable U.S. government Digital Signature Standard (DSS) uses public-key technology, but it is not a public-key cryptosystem. Digital watermarks are embedded in digital objects so that owners and perhaps end users can detect illegitimate copying or alteration. Digital watermarks can be made either "perceptible" (by people) or "imperceptible." A "fragile" watermark is damaged by image distortions and thus serves to detect alterations made after the watermark is applied. A "robust" watermark survives distortions such as trimming away most of the image and thus can serve as evidence of provenance.

Both kinds can be embedded in most varieties of digital object. Watermarks are currently of most interest for images, audio signals, and video signals. A watermark is a digital signal, added to or removed from the original object, that does not interfere unduly with the intended use of the altered object and yet carries a small amount of information. "Invisible watermarks" are imperceptible to people but can be detected by appropriate software. A technical protection service (TPS) that uses watermarking can provide a content distributor with a way to mark content before distribution and track what happens to it subsequently.

Users of works may also benefit, because successful watermark detection can demonstrate the source of the content and that it has not been altered subsequently. Even when designed to be subtle, watermarks do modify the content that carries them and therefore may be unacceptable for applications that need very high fidelity content. In a robust watermarking scheme, it is assumed that the marked object may be altered in the course of its normal use. For example, robustly watermarked images may undergo compression and decompression, filtering, scaling, and cropping.

The inputs to and outputs from a robust watermarking insertion procedure are the same as in the case of fragile watermarking. The inputs to the detection procedure are the watermarked object (which may have been legitimately altered in the course of normal use), the watermark that was inserted into the object, and the key. The detection procedure then indicates whether the object contains a mark that is "close to" the original watermark. The meaning of "close" depends on the type of alterations that a marked object might undergo in the course of normal use.

In a fingerprinting scheme, there is an additional input to the insertion procedure that depends on the recipient of the specific copy. The output is a marked object in which the mark (the fingerprint) identifies the recipient. Two different customers purchasing the same work would receive objects that appeared the same to human perception but contained different watermarks. If unauthorized copies were later found, the fingerprint could be extracted from those copies, indicating whose copy had been replicated. Digital labels can serve some of the same IP management purposes as digital watermarks.

An important difference is that no attempt is made to hide a digital label; it is intended to communicate the terms of use of a digital work and should be noticeable by readers or viewers. In its simplest form, a digital label could take the form of a logo, trademark, or warning label (e.g., "may be reproduced for noncommercial purposes only"). Alternatively, more sophisticated labeling strategies may be used. Like watermarks, labels cannot force compliance with copyright law and licensing terms.

In US, the National Office of Digital Archiving (NODA) would be responsible for developing standards and guidelines for archiving digital materials. The job of maintaining the archives should be contracted out to specialist agencies with the appropriate expertise. Once material is selected for preservation it should be kept for ever. Funding for digital archiving must come from the public sector via higher education institutions, legal deposit libraries, the funding councils and NODA itself. Legal deposit legislation should be amended to cover electronic publications and other digital material such as sound and video recordings.

The digital repositories claiming to serve an archival function must be able to prove that they are who they say they are by meeting or exceeding the standards and criteria of an independently-administered program for archival certification. The certified digital archives will have available to them a critical fail-safe mechanism, which would be a legal right. This would enable them to exercise an aggressive rescue function to save culturally significant digital information. A distributed structure, built on a foundation of electronic networks, places archival responsibility with those who presumably care most about and have the greatest understanding of the value of particular digital information objects.

Moreover, such a structure locates the economic and cultural incentives where they are most likely to prompt those preserving digital information to respond with the greatest agility to the changing digital landscape and to the shifting tides of technology. The most efficient way to ensure that digital material is archived in the UK is to extend the legal deposit legislation so that it includes electronic publications. The on-line publications as potentially the most important means of scholarly communication in the long term. In response to the British Library's proposal, the Department of National Heritage has issued a consultation paper which requested comments about the deposit of digital publications as well as many other issues to do with legal deposit arrangements. There is much literature which describes current activities and initiatives in the UK and abroad.

The National Library of Canada conducted an Electronic Publications Pilot Project (EPPP) to identify and understand all the challenges associated with acquiring, cataloguing, preserving and providing access to Canadian electronic publications. The National Library of Australia has produced a Statement of Principles on the Preservation of and Long-Term Access to Australian Digital Objects. There are eight principles covering co-operation, the role of the creator, distributed responsibility, appraisal, rights, strategies and the role of government. Principle 2 on the role of the creator states that creators of digital objects have the initial, and in some cases a continuing, role in preserving access to them. Principle 3 on distributed responsibility says that the location, selection, identification, cataloguing and retention of digital objects will be best achieved through the co-ordinated distribution of responsibilities.

The British Library expects to be a deposit library for archiving digital materials, but the question is what is the scope of the material that will be kept. It needs to consider a selection policy of digital materials as well as for hardcopy. The national library should take on more responsibility but needs resources to do this. The British Library or an agency. ...concerned that they are too closely modelling the thinking on existing deposit libraries. Creators of digital material should act responsibly. They should not set out to create material unless they think through the long-term implications.

Suspect that in practice deposit librarians will have to take responsibility for the preservation of digital material - possibly with the higher education funding councils. The present situation is that once material is of less potential value it is made more widely available. The legal deposit library structure provides a basis for digital archiving policy. Whether or not the material is physically stored in the legal deposit libraries (LDLs) is an open question, although storing in just one location is too risky. Could be stored in several locations linked to the LDLs.

The legal deposit libraries that currently exist and should not be shared out amongst lots of archives. The British Library makes the thing remote. As far as Scotland is concerned, archive material should be the responsibility of National Library of Scotland. The record industry supports the National Sound Archive and most companies deposit with it voluntarily. However it is accepted that there could be gaps in the sound archive using this system and that they should be eliminated.

Every library in UK could take some responsibility for some material. Which material needs to be dealt with by a specialist library needs serious thought. Things will get missed, no point worrying excessively about that. Much of Usenet is like the chattering in the pub but other stuff on there is useful. People will have to spend time deciding what to preserve and different kinds of organisation will preserve different type of things. There is a range of possibilities for a range of aims.

Some respondents were unable to be more specific than to say that digital archiving should be the responsibility of Government departments, the government or the public domain. Publishers keep an archive in case it is needed for further business etc. But they cannot be relied on as they are not doing it for the same reasons as an archive would. Publishers are archiving for the moment. But some CD-ROMs from the early days are gone, they have literally vanished. The publishers have a responsibility for maintaining the databases of electronic products. Each publisher should maintain own in-house archive.

Some data are being lost because no-one taking responsibility. Problem is ensuring complete coverage. Specialists and organisations with historical responsibility for archiving digital materials were also mentioned. People who have historically done it anyway. Any things held on other media are no different. Organisations which have preserved it in old media should translate their activities to new media. Legal deposit was seen by the majority of respondents as the most appropriate mechanism for ensuring that digital material is preserved.

One thinks of legal deposit. Digital material should be included in legal deposit legislation even though it is intangible. Many digital materials are genuinely new and should therefore be part of the national archive. However access to the documents by a network should be tightly controlled. Hopeful for external legal deposit will build on journal publications - move from parallel publications to electronic only publications. Legal requirements for preservation of some information. Legal deposit for long term audit requirements. There are all kinds of medical records etc that need to be preserved for a long time to study disease demographics and other databases not covered by Public Record guidelines that ought to be protected.

Assuming something is the only version and tangible (e.g. CD-ROM) each legal deposit library should have a copy. If networked, access for all six. Publishers argue there should only be a single source as it is expensive to comply. The consensus seems to be that a voluntary code is unlikely to be satisfactory, although some people felt that a voluntary system would be better than nothing, until the legal deposit legislation is changed.

There is a good record for sound material, but everything else in the UK seems to work on a statutory basis. Legal deposit would seem to be the solution, but a voluntary agreement could be tried until then. Something akin to the existing national deposit requirements for printed material - i.e. it will be necessary to rely on the publishers to ensure that material is deposited. One respondent put forward the concept of Digital Object Identifiers (DOIs). These identifiers would incorporate existing labels such as ISBNs and could also include details of rights owners.

ISWNs (International Standard Works Codes) could also be used in this context to identify publications, digital objects etc. All digital works should have a Digital Object Identifier (DOI). This is more than an identifier; it is a receptacle for other numbering systems. For example, books get an ISBN; this is one number that could go into DOI, but an ISBN doesn't tell you about author and who owns rights as a DOI would. ISWC (International Standard Works Codes) (a 'work' could be a book, digital object, film etc). ISWC could go into DOI so all objects are traceable. Where physically object is archived it does not matter.

Archaeological curators give planning permission and this can stipulate the developers ensure the results are deposited in an archive. Waste of effort to archive it twice. They would feel quite upset to know that the BL was archiving everything that they were doing. Where there is an existing data archive that is doing it well, pointless doing all the work twice. Quality judgements needed on what to archive and what not to. People working in the discipline are best placed to decide. Some way of having a central register of the strengths of particular institutions.

Co-operation needed to decide what goes where. This system could cause problems if the material is only available in one place physically because of copyright constraints. The real issue is in selecting material for the digital archive and agreeing the criteria for selection. Some materials have an infinite life and others have a limited life. There is a high management cost associated with a selective policy. It is impossible to predict the future usefulness of material. Means of moving to new media or preserving it and ability read it.

In technical terms, so many rapid changes that a generation lasts no more than 3-5 years. More than 10-15 years preservation could be a problem. Books are not locked into a technology. Now have applications which run on MSDOS. By the year 2000, finding a machine with DOS could be a problem. Some outer limit should be left to archivists. The archive material for as long as it has commercial value. With these rights go responsibilities.

Many of the respondents expressed a desire for maintenance of digital materials in a standard format without specifying the format. Whatever is the standard language so that material can be reformatted over time. Would rely on advice of technical staff. Format that meets current international standard if there is one. Should aim for international preservation standard, as was the case for microform. Ultimately need standardised format because technology is always changing. Either constantly reformat or reformat once and say we have particular format.

There is some conflict about the cataloguing of electronic material, and there have been calls for replacements for ISBN for the electronic world. Works which need to be commercially accessible should be stored in tagged format like SGML. It is now clear that the world wide web and html are so widely accepted, that if something new was developed, it would have to be made compatible with this. So we should make HTML the model. There is a problem with the publishers. They want the archived material to look and feel exactly as it was created. Publishers reputation includes the typesetting etc. The authors general perception is that being published on the web is not as prestigious as being published by a serious publisher. If their work appears as an HTML document, they could feel that their work is demeaned. If the choice is to have an archive in HTML or not at all, surely most would chose to have it.

Format should be durable and cost effective. It should not distort appearance or content of material. Should preserve a complete and accurate representation of material archived. This is the single biggest problem. In theory it would be nice to have the original material, content and delivery but he can't see how you could achieve that. Technology seems to solve the problems it creates quickly. Provided there is a demand, people will think of a way to read old technology. Information content is not all that is important; there is a lot of value in the context and way data is presented. Whatever else you do you must preserve the original bits in their unmutilated form. May be appropriate to migrate into standard form if it is reasonably priced.

But only migrate a copy, keep the original form too. We can't force publishers to deposit stuff in certain forms and unpublished it will be in whatever form the individual has. Nowadays most people use PCs or Apples. Probably there is a gap in the records when Amstrad word processors were in common use. A digital archive should be funded by the government. It should be a national responsibility. Payment should be a national responsibility.

On the one hand, a repository organisation is partly government funded, and thus has a certain responsibility for its data. However, it would not want to spend additional money for digital archiving. Libraries must make a case for funding. Government responsibility was often linked to the British Library and other deposit libraries. Many people thought the system for print publications was suitable for digital archives. Publishers should be expected to donate a requisite number of copies. Organised in the same way as at present for print.

Government departments should keep own internal records. They would also benefit from good labelling. If material has market value, then the market will pay for it. If the digital material is part of the national collection, it should be funded in the same way as any other part. Payment is open to negotiation depending on the form of deposit. The organisation of this task would keep someone in a job for life. Public domain funding as in funding of legal deposit libraries. This should apply across the board - archival and published material. For funding, otherwise identify a predominant country. The LDLs have a claim on material originating abroad and sold substantially in the UK and Ireland. This needs to be projected positively. Public domain, but not much problem in getting private sponsorship to contribute.

In the future there will be a single digital archive. The people who create the information should put aside money for its preservation. Can associate a certain cost with preserving stuff. If we don't collect income from creators, we will not be able to preserve. Information has to become self supporting. For example, academic users pay a little, pharmaceutical companies pay a lot. So complex to preserve and so expensive, we have to charge for access.

Several people thought that funding should be shared among various sources, particularly if there were to be a distributed archive. Originators and publishers need to contribute to maintenance of materials. Top-slicing or a tax to pay for this - a levy on materials which are produced or sold - like a national insurance system. For academic purposes may be worth paying for a government funded archive. Once the critical mass is reached, it will become clear that scholars and scientists should pool their resources to protect and perpetuate the corpus; the corpus, by the way, will have to be distributed and multiply redundant.

The sponsors can be government (part of the research funding budget, perhaps), universities and research institutions, and perhaps learned societies. A distributed archive would be cheaper than a central one because many of the archives already exist. The deposit libraries could make sufficient economies through more co-operation etc to enable them to fund a centralised digital archive. The J-Store model libraries started off with several million dollars in foundation money with which they did the first digitising. Then they invited academic libraries to become subscribers. They charged a large up front sum to join and a much smaller annual fee to use the archive.

There is probably only room for one J-store in the world. The agreement of the publishers is essential. In return for allowing people to access their journals through the J-store, they get their back files digitised for them. Partnership between libraries and funding bodies. Digital preservation will cost extra. Start up costs high as it is new. It is a national function therefore needs extra funding. Legal deposit libraries get extra funding. Need not be held in a library but still an extra cost.

Costs should be shared between libraries and host bodies e.g. universities and producers as it is in their interest that it should survive.) Analogy of print, cost shared between publisher and library. For each library, it should be part of core task for which they receive funding. HE sector should pay for the bits it keeps. It is not practical to charge on point of access, it should be a collective system.

Some companies now sell storage space via the Internet. They could bid for the storage aspect, so the librarian's job would only be in selecting materials and format. The British Library (BL) is currently preparing a proposal for funding an IT infrastructure to support electronic publications in the collection under the Private Finance Initiative (PFI). As part of this they will be looking at the future funding of electronic publications for posterity.

They are making a case for extension of legal deposit to electronic documents - CD-ROMS have been one of the focuses for this, but want to extend this to electronic journals, Web sites and dynamic databases. Technology is needed for this but they cannot afford this with existing resources. Estimate £20M needed. The procurement would be based on PFI funding. Several respondents have mentioned in passing the possibility of charging for the use of an archive. Preservation of scholarly knowledge, commercial value, scientific value, defence against threats.

In private information the organisation is responsible. Public information, our cultural heritage, should be funded from the public purse. Difficult because we have suffered short termism in government. Same way as for printed publications. Bearing in mind talking about audit which would not place an equal burden on all publishers. Centrally funded body in same way as for print. If nation decides it needs this for future generations and it will have to be kept long after publishers have ceased making money from selling it; it is unreasonable to expect them [the nation] to foot the cost. Libraries own funding; don't see another option than for funding to come from the repositories.

Publishers are concerned that if publications in an archive are easy to consult they may be losing potential sales. This position is magnified if the publications can be obtained via digital networking. Some publishers invest an enormous amount in a CD-ROM which will only sell about 10 copies at an enormous price, don't like the idea of it being on a network. A number of people felt that users should only have access to material if they could prove they needed to see it, and that users should have to make an effort.

The copyright concerns of trade and scholarly book and textbook and popular magazine authors and publishers are completely different from those of the authors of refereed learned serial articles; indeed, the latter are in a profound conflict of interest with the (paper) publishers of that learned serial corpus. Copyright exists to protect authors and publishers from two kinds of theft: Theft of text (through contraband reading or selling) and theft of authorship (through plagiarism, etc). Trade authors and publishers have a common interest in protecting their products from both forms of theft.

Both publishers and authors lose revenue if their joint product is stolen rather than fairly paid for. All the worse if they are re-sold under another's name. But the authors of refereed journal articles are concerned only about theft of authorship. For them, theft of their text is a victimless crime. It is precisely to be read by as many people as are interested that they publish their research in the first place. The much reduced per-page cost of electronic-only journals will not be recovered through subscriptions, site licences, or pay-per-view (the three cost-recovery models paper publishers are currently considering) but by author page charges, covered either by the author's research grants, or the author's institution, or an outright subsidy by a consortium of interested parties (governments, research foundations, institutions of research and higher learning) in exchange for a learned serial corpus that is free for all, globally, and in perpetuum.

Legal deposit repositories should not be given new powers to allow preservation. No copying of non-print material should be allowed for preservation. Copyright is different from moral rights and both are needed. Software and supporting data is an issue. Sometimes the publisher is not the owner of the copyright for the software. There are agreements with third parties which may preclude deposit arrangements.

The software producers may have to become involved and they are difficult to identify and may be outside the UK. Publisher signs an agreement with software house who agree to support technical problems. Term for the licence and publishers would not continue a licence for a product produced years ago if we no longer use that software. A library holding national archive could incur problems here as the software house has an interest. Licenses would have to be held centrally. What if software house stops trading etc.

Some software houses agree to have their code held by a central body so if they go out of business their customers have the safety net of going to the central body. Archival authority has to carry forward all the constraints on the developer like data protection. These have to be honoured, continuity of contract. PR Act might have relevance. There are other Acts that might relate to information gathered by government. Collection use and retention of things like statistics.

Several people would have been equally at home in two or more groups. In each case, participants were asked to say whether their organisation had developed a policy or strategy for digital archiving and, if so, what form this took.

Accordingly, they saw a need to separate out the repository function of bodies such as the British Library and their role of providing a document delivery service to make information more widely available. The British Library was seen as a commercial document provider which was in effect competing on unfair terms with other peoples' materials.

They felt that transfer of electronic publications could take place at the point of publication so long as there was an embargo on release to the general public. If no guarantees could be made to publishers to protect their commercial interests the alternative rehearsed was for publishers to hand over their material at the point (defined by them) at which the publication was no longer of commercially exploitable value. So long as an electronic publication was commercially exploitable they felt that it was in the publishers' interests to maintain (and retain) it.

Although the group accepted the idea of preservation for the common good, they thought that the humanistic goal of national collections being maintained and preserved as a service to scholarship was no longer tenable because of the large volume of material and high preservation costs involved. Although some types of digital publication, such as CD-ROMs were seen as sufficiently coherent to be collected and archived, others, such as Internet sites were not. Hypertext links were seen as presenting particular problems because of the difficulty of preserving the ability to link with other sites.

Contracts between archivists and information providers, as well as co-operation amongst copyright holders to permit voluntary or legal deposit, were seen as part of the necessary response to the breaking down of traditional divisions of functions between publishers and repositories. Repositories suggested that preservation and access in the future implies a requirement for an access copy and an archival copy of the data. The problem of legal deposit as it stands is that books on deposit are as accessible as any other book held by the British Library.

However, for electronic documents the same principle probably should not apply. They saw the access and preservation roles becoming much more distinct for electronic documents. Turning to large data sets, they felt that the source of the data would determine how these should be treated. Commercial publications should have strictly limited access with the emphasis on preservation. Access should be for preservation purposes only. There was felt to be a "heritage role for digital archives" and access by the academic community was seen as necessary. This was likely to lead to a number of new operating arrangements to secure appropriate access.

The Data Archive has issued CD-ROMs of data for exclusive academic use and, where appropriate, proscribes use by commercially sponsored academics. This system depends on password access and undertakings by researchers not to use the data beyond agreed terms. A single-user licence could limit access to networks, but difficulties would remain over downloading of data and its subsequent exploitation.

When rehearsing these general issues as well as in pursuing specific aspects of digital publishing (as distinct from the creation and maintenance of electronic databases and large data sets) there was a tendency for authors, distributors and other rights holders to find common cause and to express different concerns from the publishers and representatives of organisations concerned with archiving. The British Library role as an archiving organisation should be kept entirely separate from its role as a document delivery organisation.

Indeed the British Library may not be the appropriate body, in which case we need to decide who manages the process and co-ordinates the work. It is partly a question of what Government is doing. Any strategy must allow for the possibility that resources will be more limited in the future and that future archives will not be able to sustain the level of effort currently required for their management. The difficulty that the British Library or other national bodies face is that they are serving a much wider constituency with diverging interests.

Prescriptive standards in the electronic information world have failed to achieve full recognition. However the emphasis is now on 'permissive standards' such as SGML which does not tell document creators how to create the document or even what software should be used, but does result in an environment that allows exchange of information. The IT industry moves towards interoperability. At the moment downwards compatibility is not assured. There are moves towards agreement to archive in common formats but this does not address database material.

There is a need to identify standards which are most durable, to look at standards for objects or bundles of records. It is impossible to preserve formats of data so migration is important. There is no commercial advantage in trying to standardise. Technical problems are not at issue. The concerns are more strategic in nature. There is a need to develop standards with the creators of data. Part of the dissemination process considered at the start of a project should include digital archiving of data and project outputs.

The copyright issue affects much more than just "books published on the Internet" and it is important not to lose sight of other types of digital material. Does copyright apply to transient data for instance. Copyright is the key to ownership and commercial exploitation of publications. This issue needs to be sorted out. Everything will fall into place as far as publishers are concerned. Journal articles will continue to be of ongoing interest. Textbooks translated into electronic media should be regarded as separate entities.

Copyright issues become complex if digital material is modified in any way, since it can be difficult to determine who has intellectual property rights invested in a document which has been processed (for instance during data emulation to maintain the information contained in a document) or amended by someone other than the original author. It will be difficult to resolve many intellectual property issues until international legislation is introduced. The copyright issue affects much more than just "books published on the Internet" and it is important not to lose sight of other types of digital material.

A distinction was offered between commercially-minded authors who would not like versions of their work to become widely available free of charge, and academics, whose interests would be met by their work being as widely distributed as possible. British Library to develop an integrated consistent strategy for archiving digital materials. A more or less serious case was advanced for investigating the pornography industry, which possibly offers one of the most commercially successful areas of Internet commerce, where, typically, small access fees are offset by large numbers of transactions.

The concerns about copying and re-distribution of images are put to one side because of the large volume of transactions. One possible funding model is a nationally-funded system, such as the British Library model for printed books. Another approach would be to extend ISBNs to electronic publications and to charge a fee that covers future archiving costs. A third would be based on the principle that the user pays, with funds going to the archive depository or to the rights holders, or to both. Yet another possibility is to fund future archiving with a tax on current activities.

The business case for keeping archives includes protection against litigation, maintenance of corporate identity and continuity. The heritage case is for historical and academic use. If the British Library or other organisation generates revenue for document supply, then some of this money should flow back to the rights holders. In the view of the publishers' group, the handover point is when the commercial exploitation has come to an end - but this depends on how durable the commercial interest is likely to be.

Issues such as amount of usage, ease of access, cost of provision of access and of preservation need to be considered. These all help in the assessment of the commercial return. One way around this would be for the publisher to retain ownership of the deposited materials and to get a royalty on accesses to electronic documents in the same way that royalties are paid for photocopies. The caretaker approach would be to pay the British Library for keeping a document which is subsequently republished. A further concern was over transfer of ownership if a publisher wished to sell a publication that was no longer of direct interest to its portfolio. Co-operation is needed from all types of publisher.

Non-profit publishers will not be able to afford to pay for archiving, so payment for archiving should be based on the ability to pay. Some publishers could pay a third party to archive material. Alternatively they could pay the British Library if they want to exploit their data in the future. Another idea was to encourage funding by charitable trusts, as in the USA, or pump-priming to fund groups of publishers and repositories to set up a digital archive. In the past academic institutions have paid for journals by subscribing to individual titles. If archived material becomes corrupt or deteriorates because of lack of use it would not matter in a market driven system.

The system needs to be market driven. The publishers do not like the idea of top-slicing publication income to establish a national archive. The archive should be voluntary with publishers transferring material when it ceases to be of commercial value. There is a danger of not making a decision about dealing with different types of information or sources that were formerly kept in paper form. This could lead to breaks in existing series and loss of valuable historical material. With book publishing there is a natural end-point, but with electronic publishing there is always the temptation for authors to go back and alter an existing text.

Some products are open-ended, such as bibliographic databases, so different criteria are needed for archiving. Snapshotsare one suggested solution to this. The publishers' group that rights owners should make the decision to publish and the British Library should make the decision on archiving but that the publisher must decide when it is appropriate to archive material. A definition of 'out of print' was needed for electronic publications, or a new criterion to determine at what point an electronic publication was handed over for archiving - the suggested definition was 'no longer commercially viable'.

Protection against catastrophe, involving back-ups of electronic media, off-site storage of back-ups, and a strategy for keeping materials up to date, necessarily adds to central archive costs, leading the Research Libraries Group in the United States to conclude that preservation responsibilities should be distributed. However, the financial implications of preservation tend to lead to pressure for centralised storage because of economies of scale.

The description of an object, changes in storage medium and encoding of documents are all changes that may need to be controlled or recorded in some way. When a digital object is delivered to an archive there has to be a way of checking that what was sent is what is received. This process is time-consuming and expensive. Preservation is currently based on perceived need. Different archiving groups are formed where there is a common interest in preserving a cluster of information - these are defined by the stakeholders. However there is no easy way of analysing cost benefits because these fluctuate as do the different groups involved. Indexing is a key and neglected area.

The software for indexing is not well developed. In moving material from one system to another the indexing functionality can be neglected or only executed to the fairly basic level of current CD-ROMs. Electronic information is re-usable in a way in which books are not - it is inherently longer lasting. Electronic publications present a problem because it is impossible to keep track of annotations and updates. It is possible to tell if a book has been tampered with. The granularity of information will affect strategies.

A book is a single entity, whereas an electronic document could be a record a paragraph or an entire document. Paper archives are preferable for parallel publications (print and electronic). Electronic documents with enriched content should be prioritised for digital preservation. The co-ordinating role should be separated from the archiving role which should be sub-contracted or delegated to specialist agencies.

The possibility of adopting a policing role as suggested for similar bodies in other countries should be considered as a way of ensuring that the archiving bodies are properly vetted. Actual archiving bodies contracted to keep national archives will depend on a number of factors, such as regional interest, type of data held, and ownership of material. Detailed catalogue records would be the responsibility of the individual archiving agencies, because of the widely varying nature of the digital materials that are archived.

The feasibility of using a common descriptor such as a Digital Object Identifier (DOI) should be investigated. Electronic publications including text, databases, digital sound and digital video· Electronic public records - records generated electronically by public bodies in the course of their business and falling within the remit of the Public Record Acts. There is a recognition that publishers have different priorities from those of a national preservation body and for this reason it is unlikely that they would be appropriate organisations for digital archiving.

4 Networking Strategies

The computerized library system were started in the 1940's yet the first important system was designed and developed as late as 1962 only which was fully put into operation in 1964. Some libraries are already computerising, or planning to computerise, their bibliographic data on special materials. In some cases, systems are being, or have been, introduced for certain individual forms, depending on local need, eg the Library of the Western Australian Institute of Technology has a multiple-approach computer-printed catalogue for slides. At the time of writing other media have not been planned for in this particular instance.

Despite some academics' pipe dreams of an integrated systems approach, there is a lot to be said for experiment with a single medium. Problems relating to programming, computer storage, and access can be identified and solved comparatively inexpensively. A most important aspect of such an experimental project is actual use of the resultant catalogue or index. In a comparatively 'closed' situation, as in the library of an educational institution, potential users of such a system can be canvassed and their comments recorded and analysed.

When libraries reach the point of finally appreciating that so-called 'special' materials are not so special that they may be rejected as 'normal' stock, or if actually acquired hidden away and largely avoided, it should be possible for multi-library catalogue use studies to be made. From these could emerge an idea of what library clienteles really need in relation to special materials. Judging by one experiment, in Pearl River Public Library, New York, when a multi-media catalogue—and even stock-integration—policy is implemented, the users readily respond to such facilities: 'Users do like to find related materials on a given subject on one place'.

In India also, computer is being used for the acquisition, processing and controlling of periodicals. Most of these systems have the following components of records, inputs and outputs, with, however, minor variations besides converting the existing manual file onto a magnetic tape. An International Standard periodicals Number, officially called the American Standard identification Number, for serial publications which is specifically useful for periodicals checking work. This number is to consist of seven decimal digits besides an eighth check digit.

MARC I Pilot project was started in November, 1965 by the Library of Congress. The main aim of this project was to distribute Library of Congress cataloguing in a machine-readable from to various libraries for the reading materials received by them so as to facilitate them to meet the explosion of knowledge and the increasing demand for easy and quick provision of required information. The MARC II was completed in 1967 with the development of a new format capable of transferring bibliographical data to the receiving libraries. The COMARC project has been taken up by the library of Congress with the financial help from the Council of Library Resources.

The Computer Output Microfilm (COM) was developed in the U.S.A. by Stromberg Carlson Company. It used the Charactron tube for projecting the computer output onto an unexposed film at high speed. The Charactron cathode ray tube was invented in the early 1950's which was responsible for displaying the results of computer processing on the phosphor-coated face of a television screen. Later on, a microfilm was attached to the screen of a television so that the information given by a computer was recorded. This device was responsible for the invention of Computer On Microfilm.

The latest types of computers which were capable of recording more than 100,000 characters per second were responsible for the replacement of electro-mechanical line-printers were, in their turn capable of printing 1,200 lines per minute each line having a width of 132 characters. Further a COM is capable of recording photographically a full page at a time as compared to a line only printed by a line-printer. Moreover, a microfilm has another advantage over the paper in the sense that the microfilm has the capacity of storing more information in a particular amount of space as compared to that of his paper equivalent as the microfilm of 105 mm x 148.75 mm size can store 225 pages of text with the reduction ratio of 42:1 Into this computer, microfilms having 16mm or 105 mm width are fied.

The former are wound in spools or cartridges while the latter are cut into microfiche. The end product of a Computer Output microfilm is a magnetic tape which contains the requisite bibliographic information besides the concerned printing and format control codes provided for the final images. This magnetic tape afterwards enters the said computer machine thus exposing a master micro-negative through which a microfilm master is developed and duplicate copies are prepared from the negative through which a microfilm master is developed and duplicate copies are prepared from the negative.

The COM machines are being used by various libraries for other library purposes also which include the maintenance of circulation records in process ordering information for acquisition and feeding cumulation and publication of catalogues directories and yearbooks etc. The OCLC started in August 1970 is a non-profit Corporation which was originally planned to be a net-work of academic libraries but now it has more than 700 user libraries with 1200 terminal including types of libraries including one national library i.e. the national Agricultural Library. It is an line system. Its data base consists of the LC MARC records, catalogue entries contributed by its member user libraries. It is a shared cataloguing system in the real system. Its data base is more than 2.3 million out of which one-third is from LC MARC data. The system is very effective as the response time for title searches was 25-30 seconds. Since it has adapted the battelle System the OCLC enables its users at remote places to search the central catalogue by author, title and subject approaches.

Its common products include computer line-printed catalogue cards besides spine & book labels accession lists & OCLC catalogue tapes for the purpose of producing COM catalogues. In this system, an IBM 1401, an IBM 1031 data collection system and 1033 printer are used, it needs book cards and borrower's cards badges. The IBM 1401 is shared by other departments of the University. For issuing a book the book card and borrower's card/badge are inserted into IBM 1031 data collection system. If valid the printer 1033 prints a book slip to be inserted in the issued book.

The first Indian computer was developed and built in 1956 art the Tata Institute of Fundamental Research, Bombay with some imported components while the second computer was built by the University of Jadavpur, Calcutta in 1963 in collaboration with the Indian Statistical Institute Similarly the Bhabha Atomic research Centre, Bombay has developed a small but high-speed digital computer for real time applications. At present in India many public and private sector firms have started manufacturing computers. The complications of managing the sensitive and complex demands of the computer in libraries re infinite and incessant.

Coupled with the fact that the computer in the hands of those derived from English stock tends to invest them with the emotional state of a Latin behind a driver's wheel this condition accounts for the fact that, even after twenty years, library computerisation not infrequently resembles the Place de l'Etoile during rush hour. While the basic problems of freedom from careful cost control, and decisions based on institutional egofulfillment rather than users' needs are still with us to a considerable degree, whatever its degree of success, the widespread application of the computer has brought changes in the way that libraries are run that were not anticipated.

Its generalisations emerge from observations of practice in the United States, mostly in academic libraries, with some reference to practice in Australia, Canada, and Great Britain. The immediate impact on library management came with the creation of the computer unit in the library, which began in the early 1960s. Computers were introduced into libraries with all the subtlety of a spear thrust in the groin, or the crash of a satellite in a back-yard swimming pool. Their rise in library economy coincided with the post-Sputnik decade, which spewed forth on education in the United States and elsewhere a flood of gold undreamed of in human history. Unlike the River Alpheus which cleansed the Augean stables, this flood left tidy barnyards all over the land hip-deep in sharn.

In retrospect, despite the material advantages which remain as residue, the 1960s was he most destructive decade of this century. Computers came to libraries straight out of the technology of industry, and brought with them the mentality that characterized industry during an extremely confused and self-defeating period. Repeated public statements by the presidents of all major airlines agreed without exception that this airplane could not justify itself economically, but conceded they would all have to buy them because they were the latest technological development, and they had to get with it.

Nevertheless, during the 1960s the computer industry was riding high, wide, and handsome, and in the process generating some of the most repulsive personalities of the century. At one time IBM home office managers would acknowledge privately that their salesmen were completely out of control, selling the moon with each computer, and the number of bankruptcies that attended the installation of computer processes in smaller businesses was alarming. These miracle-mongers swept into university computing centers on a wave of large academic budgets and pin-headed university president, and they early brought pressure on the libraries to surrender to their lures.

Librarianship was heralded as the whale-oil industry in petroleum times, and libraries were condemned as mismanaged, neanderthal units, dark blotches on the bright electronic screen. Early specialists in library computerisation were for the most part recruited from the commercial world. They brought with them these simplistic views and attitudes and a very large burden of ignorance about library operations. They seemed to specialize in yanking fish out of water to teach them how to breathe air.

From the beginning the computer unit in libraries was viewed as a foreign body, destructive to the larger organism. In time, events proved this to be the case, and this first wave of computerisers was dashed on the rocks of its own ignorance-ignorance of library operations and the demands on them, ignorance of the complexity of computerizing bibliographic projects, ignorance of the complex variations that existed in seemingly repetitive operations.

Discouraged and discredited by repeated notable failures, this first wave left or were replaced in library operations within a few years. During their tenure, there existed nearly total antagonism between them and the library staff, which they managed to keep in turmoil nearly constantly. There was no possibility of integrating them into the library in any managerial sense. The positive result of their failures was an understanding of the high degree of complexity involved in computerizing library operations. The second wave of library computer specialists as kind of rebound tended to be librarians who had some experience with programming.

In most cases, they did not have exposure in depth to an understanding of the computer, generally had not worked in other kinds of computer operations, and very few of them had high skills as programmers. They generally worked together with programmers from industrial backgrounds. On the whole the shortcoming of this generation of computerisers was inadequate programming skill, and, with the reduction of library budgets, in house-computer staffs largely disappeared in the early 1970s, although the last large staff of its kind persisted at the University of Maryland until 1978. Although this second wave of specialists was far less antagonistic to librarians, they still were held at a considerable distance, partly because they were thrust into library operations by library directors and partly because of the long drawn out agonies inflicted to their colleagues by programming methods that they prevailed.

The computer unit was still something 'out there', and if it no longer was engaged in guerilla warfare with the library staff, it nevertheless seemed to work largely at night in mysterious ways, and to slip things into operations that were not completely understood, often not needed, and even worse full of what were called 'bugs', for which there never seemed to be any truly effective exterminator. Though no longer considered the enemy, the computer unit existed for the most part despite the library staff, and could have done just as well, or badly, as a department of the university computer center.

There are few other agencies in the spectrum of human affairs so constantly involved in change. But at least until quite recently, librarians tended to be discerning, and if the tool or machine was not obviously useful it had to prove itself before being accepted. The fact is that computer efforts in libraries from 1958 to 1970 contributed almost nothing to library computerization except disruption of library processes, fantastic waste of money, and a heritage of bitterness through arrogance that has disappeared only in recent years. The Ohio State University Library circulation system is the only significant in-house computerized system that has remained more or less intact until the present day, and it came on line late in 1970.

By the end of 1970 OCLC was still in a batch card production system, BALLOTS (now ARLIN) still in its programming stage, the University of Chicago system, (offspring of the atomic bomb) was still under cloak-and-bagger cover behind vault doors, and MARC (the dinosaur with tiny brain that may yet devour us all) was still building up to solidity. The first interactive bibliographical system MEDLINE, which began in February 1972, was, in retrospect, the only highly successful library computer operation developed up until that time.

The achievements in library computerisation, then, are the product of the last seven years, and it is useful to speculate the changed conditions that made them deviate into sense and begin the Modern Age in library computerization, for which any sane operation would have waited before plunging. First and most important of all was the radical drop in library support that began to hit us in 1970 and has increased to the present day. It shook out the monkeys from the orange crop, and within three or four years stamped out library computerisation as cottage industry. The fact, blatantly obvious in the failures of the sixties, that skilled computer programming is one of the rarest commodities in the world (and rarely, seen in a library setting), began to be recognized, and we looked for help to the few large computer operations outside where it seemed to have focussed.

In US, the development in the Library of Congress of a totally computerized cataloguing system, which came very slowly and at a cost that no one has ever dared to look at, for fear that it would overthrow the national government, but with national implications. With a new set of props under their foundations, libraries could now look sensibly, with much smaller resources, at what they could produce locally, with programming done outside the library, and the present status of the computer unit and its relationship to the management structure of the library emerged. It tends to exit in two conditions. In one condition the computer unit controls decisions on library computerisation, with the advice of concerned departments, and is itself the equivalent of a department.

In the other condition, control over computerization is dispersed among the library departments, and the computer specialist provides centralized technology as a staff officer of the library director. Neither condition is totally satisfactory, and different kinds of tensions result from each. The computer unit or computer specialist in either case represents a new type of power level within the library organization. It is central to the entire operation, a pivotal unit, with no counterpart in previous library history. It can impose changes by design or inadvertently on departments with which it is not working directly, through the interaction of parts of systems and how they are affected by adjustments in the system.

The computer unit, moreover, almost always reports directly to the upper library administration, generally to the director, and while there are valid reasons for this relationship, it nevertheless places the unit in a privileged organisational relationship. These two factors cause a change in peer relationships between the computer staff and the rest of the library staff, which are altered further by the mysterious nature of what computer specialists do, procedures which are amenable to simple examination or review by no one. The computer specialist is never as fully integrated into the library structure as other unit heads can be.

For these reasons and others, the most successful computer units seem to be those headed by a librarian, with extensive knowledge of library procedures, who has accumulated the requisite systems and programming knowledge, although we know one spectacularly successful exception to this rule. Computerization has changed many relationships between departments in libraries. Its largest effect is the tilt in power balance between technical processes and public services divisions, which had been reasonably evenly distributed previously, in favour of technical processes. Evidence of this shift is seen in the emergence in the past five years into high levels of library administration, including the directorship, of librarians whose career had been in technical processes, formerly a rare occurrence.

Within the divisions the independence of the separate units has been considerably loosened. Departments formerly based on rather clearly defined functions have now had those functions changed on the basis of new procedures generated outside of their unit, and to a larger extent than ever before the library organization is beginning to be described in terms of processes that are heavily overlapping in their reach.

Boundaries have been blurred, and tensions have arisen over control of various aspects of computerization, such as the nature of processes and the demands they will impose on the department, the kind of hardware and software to be used. The nature, location, control, and scheduling of computer terminals are often a matter of bitter dispute. Like elevators, they are far more economical if arranged in banks, but their cost strictly limits the number obtainable.

All of these factors have greatly increased the amount and constancy of negotiation necessary to conduct relationships between departments. A typical battle in American libraries occurs in locating the bank of OCLC terminals, which are likely, especially early in the use of the system, to be used by cataloguing, acquisitions, serials, inter-library loan, documents, reference, and even rare book librarians. While the early promise by computer-flappers in the early sixties was that every man could be his own terminal, with access to world information easily achieved by this point in time, there are a limited number that can be obtained by a library because of their cost.

The matter of cost is the most frustrating aspect of the entire range of computers in libraries. We know that it can do wonders for us in the hands of competent computer managers. The computer, in fact, presents the only longterm solution to the two most pressing problems in the entire range of librarianship-short-life paper of books, which is rapidly heading for shorter life with economic trends in paper manufacturing that are irreversible, and even shorter-life bindings (ironically called 'perfect bindings') for books, about ninety percent of which are held together by plastic smeared on the edges of loose pages at the present time. These crack after seven or eight circulations, and twenty years from now any library committed to preserving books over time will be a mass of loosely-tied sheets.

The promise of locating terminals everywhere, which of course is the highest desideratum in any information system, cannot begin to be realized, either now or in the long-term future in the declining state of library budgets. The future will see us with fewer terminals, rather than more, and struggles between departments for control will become even more acute. All departments affected by computerisation (which includes most of them) become dependent on outside technology experts with the introduction of the computer, and this has markedly reduced their autonomy.

While this often is not an entirely bad thing to happen, because departments can become rigid, it is futile to assume that basic decisions about what a department is doing and how it does it can be made better outside the department than in it, or better when having to accommodate the needs of other departments than when decided entirely on internal needs. An automated circulation system, for instance can have an impact of considerable depth on the budget, priorities, and scheduling of acquisitions, cataloguing, and collection management, that is to say, it can rearrange their use of staff and funds, and churn up long standing policies that have emerged from years of negotiation and adjustment between departments within the library and the entire range of academic experts on a campus. The affected departments do not expect the circulation department to have an impact on them, and there is a tendency to resist or reject the new demands that should logically result from circulation information analysis.

Nowhere in the costing of computer operations in a library is any account made of the cost of the time required for negotiations and the toll of these tensions on efficiency of departments placed in this new and far less secure matrix of organizational relationships, but it has to be a noticeable cost. Branches pose special problems to the main library in any dispersed system, and they are a special element in the interdepartmental relationship changes that follow computerization. Branches tend to go their own way to a large degree. They have their own support constituency in their academic specialists on a campus whom they can bring to bear on the library ad instruction. They are not constantly viewed, as internal library departments are likely to be, by staff passing through the library.

Changes in their conditions to service can occur without being detected by the main library, and they impose large demands on the main library's central services for processing and information. With computerisation, the branches become far more dependent on the main library. While they may gain access to the records of the entire library system collection, which is highly desirable, this may be in the form of microfiche catalogues which they may not like. They also will lose their card catalogues.

However, centralization of the locus of collection records, if on line to branches with provision for defining whether materials are available, can remove a large burden of the curse of branch libraries to students, who are driven mad by the dispersal of books among libraries for reasons that seem insane and on a rationale that defies acceptance. The branch libraries under a campus-wide computerized circulation system like that of Ohio State University, become access points for searching the entire system and reserving books for pick-up, greatly broadening the use of materials in all the other branches and in the main library.

The intolerable delay of a minute by telephone to determine current periodical holdings, which led nationwide to branch library check-in records duplicating the main serials record, yields to sense when the delay is only ten seconds by computer. Computer application tends to standardize methodology in the branches, making transfer of staff easier and cheaper. In public library branches that must respond to rapid change in public demand for the most recent books, easy turnover of book stock is possible with a centralized computer catalogue and computerized check-out of books to the branch, instead of local card catalogues. It is also possible to generate management information about the branches for the library administration that will inform it more sensitively on a timely basis of what goes on in the branches, making them more amenable to central policy control.

In general, computer applications tend to make the branches less autonomous, but in the near future we should see the processing of all their materials return to the branches, as it is facilitated by the system. Although a the present time few libraries have more than a few operations computerized, throughout the land most library departments somewhere or other have tried their little trotters at some from of automation. Some of the wildest computer money was squandered by enthusiastic fools with keypunched brains in converting shelflists to machine readable form with no foresight about what was required for multiple use of these records, and no insight into the requirements for proper bibliographical standards.

Enormous sums of money were spent in keypunching, and the resulting carloads of IBM cards lying around in closets throughout the land have scarcely been used and are mostly unusable. In US, the University of Toronto library reports being confronted by "five separate files which had strong family resemblances but were not really compatible," resulting from keypunching that went back to 1965. Before the volume of MARC records at the Library of Congress grew large enough to dominate the scene, most computerized cataloguing records fell far short of standards for reasonable bibliographical access. The data base at OCLC still suffers from the fact that early entries into their computer from some libraries were not subject to quality control.

At present computerized cataloguing information is produced almost exclusively by the few large central on-line data bases and bought by local libraries, who enter any local records not already in the data base as well as deriving records from it. When these data bases reached the critical mass that met most of the demands for current cataloguing in smaller libraries, their use increased greatly. This point was reached when two or three of the larger research libraries joined the system and began adding their records to those generated by the computer center.

The rapid formation of regional networks with multiple members was accelerated by the need for smaller libraries to have contracting, access lines, and hardware procured by a central agency, and membership in such centers as OCLC has more than doubled in the past four years. The ease of joining these systems has tended to slow the development of local on-line mini- and micro-computer systems, which pose many problems identical to those handled to badly during the first decade of library automation.

Because of the mass of information in the card catalogue, in the development of local on-line systems the card catalogue may be the first to be converted or the last. The impact of automated cataloguing on the staff of cataloguing departments has been beneficial, since one of fits early results was the eradication of inefficient hand-cataloguing operations, of which there were many. The reason why libraries that joined OCLC early could show immediate cuts in staff was that many of them had cataloguing departments with very low productivity.

Professional cataloguers who had been performing work easily accomplished by the support staff, practice that had stubbornly outlived the surge of acquisitions of the 1960s, were immediately obsolete and professionals now are restricted to original cataloguing. Except in those libraries expect in replicating inefficiencies, where professional cataloguers are used at computer terminals to summon catalogue cards. There has been retraining of the support staff, and some reduction of total staff in the cataloguing processes. Radical staff cuts in previously efficient cataloguing departments have not occurred.

On the managers of cataloguing departments there have been new demands requiring considerable ability to understand technological processes, radical new demands for training programs, increased demands for supervision and work-flow adjustment, and infinite patience in coping with the peculiarities, changes, and failures of the on-line centers. These managers, once proudly suspicious of the flawed nature of humankind which generates the chaos in which they flourish, have now become total believers in the new magic-that once the button on the terminal is pushed the catalogue cards will inevitably come and that all the cards required in the card-set will inevitably be present in the alphabetical cumulations they receive from remote computer centers.

These changes have resulted in cataloguing processes that are more expensive than efficient hand-cataloguing, but which produce much faster processing of the current flow of acquisitions to the shelves. The cataloguing department has become a much more central department than formerly, because it is the closest in need to the data base terminals. Its high priority demands on these terminals make it a host department to other departments using the terminals in most libraries. This department has experienced the largest change through computerization of any large library department.

Processing department, which is often absorbed into the cataloguing department, spent most of its time before computerized cataloguing maintaining files from which were drawn the bibliographical base for production of catalogue cards, an din producing the proper number of catalogue cards, in a variety of ways. This process has been entirely eliminated, and the largest cuts in staff produced by library automation have occurred in this unit. There still remains the task of filing cards in the various library catalogues, and the magnitude of this task is leading to the closing of library card catalogues in the large research libraries throughout the land. No satisfactory substitute for the card catalogue has yet been found short of local production of catalogues in microform or on-line access to local computerised catalogues, a process that is still excessively expensive.

This new condition has reduced the requirement of extremely high typing skills and high bibliographical skills in the staff of this department, making replacements easier to select, in a unit that characteristically has a high staff turnover. One of the earliest applications of the computer to libraries, often generated by self-seekers outside of the library was to bookkeeping records of the order department, which are fairly simple records subdivided into allocations of the book budget by categories.

While this is a simple, commonplace computer operation in business, we have seen more of them in libraries that did not seem to work effectively than one could imagining. By now, most of them have been straightened out, but in libraries that programmed their own systems, departure of the librarian programmer has generally left behind an undocumented system that had to be reprogrammed. These systems involve payment of vendors through code numbers assigned to each vendor, and payments to the wrong vendor occur not infrequently.

At present the on-line cataloguing data banks are used by order departments for verification, which has greatly speeded up the search process. New processes have required staff retraining, but there has not been much change in the size of the staff. However, the nature of the searching, which formerly required educated, intelligent, and bibliographically skilled staff has changed, making it possible to recruit at a lower level of skill for these positions although they have not yet been downgraded in most libraries. The new demands on the manager of this department require heavy interaction with the computer specialist, negotiation for the use of terminals controlled by others, and heavy dependence on outside sources for program maintenance, re-programming, failures of the reporting schedule, and incorrectly paid bills. Since computerized circulation records essentially involve manipulation of numerical data, they were among the very earliest to be automated. Like everything caught up in the forefront of the wild enthusiasm of early computerization, the butchery that resulted often made even computers run blood.

At one time information generated at this point was made the basis for all other computer applications in the library from cellar to attic, with disastrous results. The library at the present time almost always depends on an outside computer for processing its data. It is not rare for these operations to wipe out completely the entire circulation record. While this can be regenerated to some degree of approximation by using previous computer tape records, there is no possibility of ever recovering completely from such a disaster.

One library was about to shorten its circulation period from three weeks to two weeks, only to discover that the outside agency that handled its data was about to change to a new computer. This required total re-programming of every operation serviced by that computer, and two-and-a-half years later, when the computer operation had been converted and the library circulation system had worked its way into the re-programming schedule, it was possible to change that circulation period.

A prime example of that fact that although the computer initially can be a great accelerator of change, once imposed it becomes a powerful agent against change. The difficulty of managerial control over programmers was demonstrated in one system that generated a daily Computer Output Microfilm circulation record. Although very small high school and public libraries that could in no way justify it either on functional or cost ground computerized their circulation records to get with it, there were nevertheless valid reasons for computerizing this operation in larger libraries.

At present, most computerized circulation systems are remnants of local programming (some still the relicts of wild-and-woolly local library programming), and they yearn toward on-line systems, the simple and obvious condition for the solution of circulation record problems. Few can afford them. In the interim, light-pen collector systems are being used more and more, but instead of using packaged software programs (with known effects and predictable costs) these often are subjected to local programming, with all its attendant evils.

Computerised circulations systems, once past the gargantuan task of keypunching cards for each book in the library, have eliminated the staff formerly used for filing and overdues, and have greatly eased the space-crush at the central circulation desk. They require very little staff training, and have imposed no great demands or the department manager. Except at times of re-programming, when dislocations in the records (until de-bugged) are so frequent and irrational that he must become a psychiatric social worker to avert hysteria on his staff, and an international diplomat to smooth the ruffled senses of library users. Once the shortcomings of computerized circulation systems have been absorbed by the manager, this operation becomes easier to manage than previously, since it involves far fewer workers, and so sizeable new problems.

Larger libraries tend to subscribe to two or three of the most comprehensive in their fields of greatest demand with others added, as specialities and finances dictate. They are all extremely expensive, and the main-line bibliographical services are computerized versions of printed indexes with only slight extension of their coverage. Their virtue is the saving of time involved in manual searching of indexes, a factor of importance to advanced research workers. Costs of using them tend to be passed on to the user, which eliminates use by the ordinary library user or by the staff, useful as these services could be in routine reference work.

They require extensive training, study, and experience in depth of veteran professional reference librarians, preferably educated in a discipline (science, social science) in the area on which the data base focuses. There is a certain amount of prestige connected with this retrieval that enhances the status of the librarian engaged in it. The use of COM catalogues, spread around the university, or on-line catalogues with multiple terminals, reduces the use of reference departments for card catalogue assistance, which is provided at the other access points in the system. The extension of reference power that will be possible with the advent of on-line catalogue information accessible in all the ways now possible at the card catalogue, and with expansion of ways of approaching the data base, must wait for the day when libraries can afford such services.

The added computerised services have been assumed by reference departments without additions to staff and at a time when, indeed, public service staffs are being cut all over the country. They have required transfer of skills from the lower level users (typically at the student level) to the research level user at a time when services to students is deteriorating at an alarming rate. They have imposed no perceptible burden to managers of reference departments, and have equipped them with the new magic carpet-a computer terminal, to achieve which some good librarians give up librarianship.

In any sensible social or economic condition, decisions about whether to use technology or what kind to use depend entirely on what you are trying to achieve and what you should buy to attain the largest library service at the level of quality you require. In a condition where magic and witchcraft predominate in any of their manifold forms the arcane rituals must be applied, though they kill the body. With the radical decline of personal confidence of librarians who shudder at the thought of being labelled obsolete, not 'with it', defenders of 'the old manual system' and other cock-a-many nonsense, the magic words branded on our bosom are 'change' (for all changes are obviously good) and 'technology'.

Like the Boeing 747, the computer must be used in library processes, no matter how much more costly or what its degree of success, merely because it has been invented. But once it is used, the Director is not off all of his hooks. There were more sound and mature directors squeezed out of their positions in the late 1960s in disputes over computerization than you could count. Ironically, they were fired for being on either side. If they did not apply the computer, because they saw the messes in library computerization throughout the land, they were pressured by the local computer boys and the administration; if they did apply the computer, with the level of results usually attained at that time, they were pressured by their agonized staff and users. The budget squeeze of the 1970s made university administrators look at the costs of what they referred to as 'free' computer time, and prudence in approaching the computers was allowed.

However, the directors of research libraries are heading into a major decision with very long term implications for the entire library, depending on which cataloguing data base they will choose to contract with. In some libraries this also will involve major commitments of budgets. This decision now emerges from what seemed to be a simple decision four years ago of where they would buy on-line computer-produced catalogue cards. Outside sources, as of this date, cannot to all of the work in the library, and dealing with local application of what is always an unruly technology presents the director with some of his most difficult problems. In many ways the director is the prisoner of his staff, dependent on them for information to cope with the bewildering range and numbers of complex problems that continually expand before him.

In the case of the computer unit, however, this is virtually impossible, leaving this operation to a large extent on the honour system. The director is far more dependent on the technologist's expertise than on any other unit head. For reasons which range from frivolous to profound, the computer head's decisions are questioned by more peers in the library than are those of any other librarian. The director is left to unsnap these department rivalries. In many cases, the internecine disputes lead to hiring an outside consultant to help make decisions on a level above the emotional entanglements within the staff.

The ability to manage with any degree of sensitivity the development of a computer program in terms of its time-table, its economy of machine time and storage, its documentation (so others can run it), the avoidance of program-play (a speciality of professional programmers), and cleanness of the program to minimize misfires is almost never within the scope of the director. Someone else controls it, in the library or elsewhere. Consequently, there is a looseness of control over the computer unit that would be inconceivable in the case of any other department. And yet, this relationship is crucial in a library, especially in one dedicated to rapid change, since application of the computer can produce more change in less time than any other factor in existence short of total budget withdrawal. If the changes are not good, the resulting difficulties can take five years to repair.

For all these reasons, some of the younger library directors who are beginning to emerge here and abroad are those with deep experience in computer applications. Management information, which the computer can generate by the mile, is not used very much and generally not used effectively at any managerial level in libraries at the present time. The ability of the computer to identify exactly which books have circulated is not often used at a time when radical constriction of books budgets requires precise information about what kinds of materials to buy. Many of the director's problems with the computer, including early detection of poor performance, could be relieved by one-line information systems, whose costs still place them a considerable way in the distance.

Smaller operations, such as public library branches, with small demands for information storage can move to on-line micro-computers more easily than large and complex libraries with huge information demands, and to some extent this is happening, although movement into computerization by American public libraries has been very slow. A sizeable portion of the library budget has been transferred to computerization and the staff to run it. Almost without exception, this constitutes additional costs, even after deducting cost savings resulting from the change.

This looseness of careful cost control in such decisions is best illustrated in the application of the computer to new academic libraries that began in the 1960s and even now are drastically short of collection strength, without regard for what could have been done with the money by forgoing computerization. This use of computerization as a public relations cosmetic to disguise basic inadequacy is illustrated in such cases as the Australian library 1,500 miles from the nearest substantial collection, supporting ten Ph.D. programs on a collection of 60,000 volumes, which boasted of being computerized up to the ears.

These are computer diversions from library inadequacies. The sloppy management, or non-management of the costs of computers in libraries is not as bad today as it was ten years ago, but in the present state of library funding here and abroad, many of us should have been hung long ago for some of the things we have done. The lynchings still may take place. Computer costs are now visible enough in many library budgets to be targets for cuts by university administrations in the budget squeeze besetting the academic world.

Computerisation tends to divert more money into equipment than formerly occurred, and as we become more dependent on on-line access from multiple consoles this will become increasingly the case. As computer budgets grow larger and state financing tightens as is likely to be the case in most states in the next few years they will be prime targets for a sweeping cut.

Archiving and Preserving E-journals

In many ways, archiving and preserving e-journals will be

dramatically different from what has been done for paper-based journals. In the paper era, there was large-scale redundancy in the storage of journals. Many different institutions collected the same titles. The copies of journals being saved for future generations were the same copies being read by the current generation of users. Many of the things that helped maintain journals for the long term were not differentiated from what a library did to provide current services.

Other than in the case of preservation microfilming and the odd instance of shared book storage facilities, there was little conscious coordination of preservation activities, and in fact a level of redundancy was expected and thought useful. The common service model for e-journals is quite different than that for paper journals. Most e-journal access is through a single delivery system maintained either by the publisher or its agent. There is little replication, and only a few institutions actually hold copies of journals locally.

Libraries can fulfill their current service requirements without facing the issues involved in the preservation of the resources. Further, in the digital realm the issues involved in day-to-day service are quite different from those involved in long-term preservation. The issue of long-term archiving and preservation of e-journal content has become one of increasing importance. Specifically because of archiving concerns, many research libraries continue to collect paper copies at the same time they pay for access to the electronic versions. This dual expense is not likely to be sustainable over time.

Publishers are finding that authors, editors, scholarly societies, and libraries frequently resist moving to electronic-only publication because of concern that long-term preservation and access to the electronic version is uncertain. Publishers and subscribers, and publishers and archives, have formal contractual relationships; does there need to be a formal relationship between archives and subscriber? An archive that keeps its content dark poses less of a threat of competition to the publishers with whom it is working.

A dark archive will also be relieved from having to maintain a current user interface, with all of the bells and whistles that users have come to expect, and from the complex task of maintaining information on who has access to what content. On the other hand, insuring that content that is never used remains sound and free from degradation will be challenging. Keeping records of who has the right to access what and implementing appropriate access control mechanisms that recognize differential rights to various archived objects would be a major operational challenge.

At first hearing, most people assume that e-journal archiving is basically concerned with the content of journal articles. Indeed, while articles are the intellectual core of journals, in fact e-journals contain many other kinds of materials. For example, few if any e-journals provide a list of who was on the editorial board for an issue published a year or two ago. Another difficult content type is advertisements. Advertisements are, of course, frequently not tied to any given issue, and they change over time with the business arrangements of the publisher.

In some cases, advertisements are specific to certain populations, and what advertisements you see depend on who or where you are. Deciding what of all that is seen on e-journal sites today should be archived and maintained will require careful consideration by archives, publishers, and scholars.Should content be normalized? The variety of formats of digital objects in an archive will affect the cost and complexity of operation.

Many e-journal publishers encode article content in SGML or XML (or plan to do so soon). Most publishers create their own DTD (or modify an existing DTD) to suit their specific needs and delivery platforms. An archive might choose to normalize all such marked-up documents into a common DTD, reducing the complexity of documentation, migration, and interface software. Normalization and translation always involve the risk of information loss.

In archiving there may well be a difficult trade-off between information loss and reduced complexity and cost of operation. The OAIS model uses the concepts of "information packages," that is, bundles of data objects and metadata about the objects that are the unit of deposit, storage, and distribution by an archive. The model allows transformations to be done as objects move from one type of package to another. If as expected any given publisher is depositing content into a number of different archives, and any given archive is accepting deposits from a number of different publishers, standardizing the format of "Submission Information Packages" may reduce operational cost and complexity for both communities. A key element in digital preservation is maintaining the usability of digital objects in current delivery technology as the technical environment changes over time.

This process is usually assumed to be one of "format migration," that is, the transformation of objects from obsolete to current formats, although it could also be carried out through emulation, that is, maintaining current programs capable of emulating older technology, thus rendering obsolete formats. Whatever the method, the cost of preservation will be sensitive to the number and types of formats in an archive. E-journals can contain a very wide range of technical formats, particularly as they begin to accept digital files created during the process of research that help validate, supplement, or further explain the basic content of articles.

Whether it will be practical for archives to maintain current usability for such a diverse range of formats is far from clear. It is possible that archives will need to differentiate between formats where usability will be maintained and formats for which the archive will insure that the bits are maintained as deposited and that whatever documentation exists about them is kept useable for future "digital archeologists". Who pays what? Archiving and preserving e-journal content will cost money. Perhaps the most important single financial issue is how archiving can be implemented to minimize the cost to the community.

Over time, many different parties can be expected to contribute to the effort. Certainly for one-time or episodic expenses, sources such as foundations or government funding programs are likely sources of support. But archiving is a continual process, with expenses incurred on an on-going basis. So, a reasonably secure, continuous funding source is required. It has been suggested by some that archives could support themselves through fees to users for access.

However, if the purpose of an archive is to provide failsafe access rather than daily service, this model will not provide on-going operational funding. Archiving is a form of insurance, and as with insurance one experiences the expense on an on-going basis but experiences the benefit only occasionally. Expecting to recover the cost of archiving only at the point at which access to the archived content is necessary is impractical.

Such incidents will be rare and randomly timed, whereas the cost of archiving will occur from the first day of deposit. Another widely-discussed option is for archiving to be funded by governments through the agency of national libraries or similar bodies, particularly for materials subject to copyright deposit. This may indeed be a good model for support of some archiving, but it is unlikely to be sufficient. Not every country will be equipped or financially willing to assume archiving responsibilities.

More importantly, one archival agency for a work is insufficient. While digital archiving need not involve the scale of redundancy that we had in the paper era, some redundancy is highly desirable. There is too great a danger that a single incident, decision, or mistake can destroy what has been archived. A sound archiving model should involve multiple archival copies in the hands of different organizations, subject to different laws and political influences, and dependent upon different technical infrastructures and preservation activities. For archives lacking independent funding such as governments can provide, the most attractive funding model may well be one that involves the deposit of funds to maintain materials at the same time the materials themselves are deposited.

Such a "dowry" would insure the growth of funds in proportion to the growth in responsibility. Dowry funding might come through the agency of the publisher, but its ultimate source is most likely to be the subscribers to the archived journals. This funding could be made visible through the means of an "archiving surcharge" added to subscription fees, or it could be simply wrapped into the budgets of publishers and/or journal owners. The centralized e-journal delivery model pursued by many publishers does not account for the core function of archiving, and introducing it back into the model can be viewed as a natural cost element of electronic publishing. Of course, the general scholarly community is the key beneficiary of archiving.

Subscribers and scholarly societies can serve as surrogates for that community in the realm of e-journals, and a cost model based on funding from such sources is not unreasonable. Many aspects of publishing are being transformed by the arrival of the World Wide Web and its facility to distribute information electronically. For journals, the transformation has barely begun. A large number of journals are now available in electronic form of some kind, but otherwise little has changed. Recently, one leading publisher reportedly described the growth of electronic journals based on the portable document format (PDF) as the "first frontier" facing journal publishers just a couple of years ago. The second frontier is the emergence of links, he went on to say.

Judged by this measure alone, journals may have appeared on the Web but have yet to adapt to it. Publishing may have changed, but readers probably experience little difference between Web-delivered journals and, in many cases, their print originals. New and better features that can be supported electronically are now being demanded by users, however, supported by librarians, as the price of acceptance of these new products. Of these new features, links are one of the most important. Since 1995, the Open Journal project has been applying original software tools and techniques to support flexible linking in e-journal applications, based on selected journals which were available electronically but which were are not all exclusively electronic.

In doing so, the project foretold the impact that links will have. Links are not a superficial feature of the Web, nor are they simple add-on features for e-journals. Links have the power to alter the character of journals fundamentally, most obviously in the development of "distributed publishing" in which users can find items of interest irrespective of the publisher. Ultimately, distributed publishing may transform the way in which individual documents are compiled by sharing components or "objects", figures say, from different sources, and by using network-based software processes, or services, to enhance presentation.

In practical terms, the Open Journal approach involves four components, respectively, linking, resources, formats and location. The link service used in the project was developed as a research tool at Southampton University and was based on technology that has been commercialised, under other names, for other applications. It quickly became apparent from project users that whatever you call the underlying linking tool, it is the functionality that counts, and that functionality must be presented to users as transparently as possible. The functionality, and the novel twist in this case, is that the links are added to documents that have been requested by users as they are downloaded.

Up-to-date links are published within the document upon delivery rather than authored in typical HTML style because they are served by the link service separately from the document source and added on the way to the client via a proxy server. Resources of a wide variety of types, from primary journals to databases, were generously provided by a group of twelve publisher partners most of which supported the project throughout its full period and some of which continue to work with the project developers. The linking tools will be compliant with the linking component of XML, an important new format for Web documents that emerged during the latter months of the project.

Full compliance will be formalised following publication of the XLink and XPointer standards. Recognising that it will never be possible to serve the information needs of users from single resources or single Web sites, a vital feature of this approach was that links could be applied to documents wherever they are on the Web—the distributed journal scenario again.

Three demonstrator journals were produced in the subject areas of cognitive science, biology and computer science. These areas and the core journal resources contained within the respective Open Journals were effectively defined by the interests of the research teams and the publishers that supported the project.

Development was further informed by subject specialists, including researchers, teachers and librarians, in each of the areas. For the purposes of this analysis, however, it is more convenient to consider the demonstrator Open Journals from the viewpoint of the linking features they highlighted. The three main link types in this application can best be described as citation links, keyword links, and PDF links.

Citation links act on references contained within papers. Print journals are constrained to work backwards in time, citing earlier works; electronically, links can also point forward in time, to later papers that have cited the one being viewed, or even to later papers that have cited any of the references contained within that paper. The influences on a work and its own influence can thus be tracked. How completely a thread can be tracked in this way depends on the number of citation links that can be presented, which in turn depends on the scale of the data that can be linked.

Given the small size today of the electronic full-text archive, citation linking on a meaningful scale requires a secondary database of abstracts. The project was fortunate to be able to work with data provided by the Institute for Scientific Information (ISI) from its citation indexes. These indexes not only include abstracts from papers but the references too, and this is the basis of its distinctive services, now translated to the company's Web of Science. Working with a much smaller, but still substantial (500 MB), data set than Web of Science, the project demonstrated forward and backward linking within the secondary data but went further, extending the linking capability to remote but accessible full-text journals. For those journals it was shown that references could be linked—where the data set allows; in this example the data set was not big enough for comprehensive linking—to the secondary data or, potentially, to other full-text journals independently of the established authoring and publication process.

An important and successful component of citation linking was a software-based citation agent developed for use in the project. This agent recognises reference data within a downloaded paper, matches the citations against a pre-indexed database of abstracts, and links the references to entries in the database where matches are found. All of these actions are performed in "real time" as the requested paper is downloaded. Conceived as an autonomous processor, the agent was partitioned as a "library" of functions to allow it to be integrated with other programs. In the project, this approach was used to enable the agent to be used with the link service and PDF software.

While the Open Journal project emphasised text recognition, matching, and linking, other projects are concerned with software agents that can find cited works on the Web, and improved search services and parsing of other document formats to build automatic and comprehensive citation indexes. Another approach to serving links separately from documents is Hyper-G, an electronic publishing package based on a Web server with an object-oriented distributed network database and a separate link database. Hyper-G has been used in journal projects with Springer-Verlag and Academic Press. In one sense, serving links in this way is a rough-and-ready but practical method for implementing relationships, represented explicitly as links, between documents from different sources.

This is a flexible approach but because no control is exercised over the documents, the links can be unstable and need to be rigorously mantained. At the other end of the spectrum, an ideal application-independent and stable way of identifying documents or their components might be the Digital Object Identifier. Publishers to have prototyped applications represented in the the gallery of the International DOI Foundation include Academic Press, Elsevier, Springer-

Verlag, and Wiley. The DOI is not yet an accepted standard. and to become so would require wide agreement. While links simply provide access to works, however, the DOI has a more demanding remit: "The intent of the (Association of American Publishers) AAP's Enabling Technologies Committee (which designed the DOI) was to support copyright protection, while ameliorating inconvenience to users, by supporting technology that promotes interoperability'. It is not clear that these objectives can be easily reconciled without compromising user access.

There are also concerns about possible limitations, such as restricting organizations that are permitted to assign DOIs to "legitimate" publishers. Between the DOI and link serving is Hellman's proposal for the Scholarly Link Specification Framework (SLinkS) which applies DOI-like identifiers to documents from different publishers but controlled via an intermediary service. It is already clear from a number of publishing arrangements that the electronic scholarly literature will be dominated by cross-linking on citations between different journals and services. ISI Links has been announced as its means of mediating citation linking between Web of Science, collaborating publishers, and subscribing institutions.

Linking applications where links are applied between different journals and documents directly managed by a single publisher have been described for the BioMedNet service, HighWire Press and the Institute of Physics. Some Web-based abstracts services enable third-party users to create links to entries in these sites. Keyword linking is more contentious than citation linking. Keywords are a means of classification that does not automatically translate to linking on the same scale as citation linking.

Keywords are often created by the authors of papers, and therefore may not always be compiled systematically. Publisher and editor intervention can help by formalising the terms selected, especially in structuring the terms in a hierarchy. As a result, however, indiscriminate linking based on keywords can produce results which appear not to match authorial intent and produced, early in the project's first demonstrations, some adverse reactions from users. Given the ubiquity of keywords within quality journals, and the frequency with which terms might appear given their position in the classification hierarchy, it became a relatively simple task programmatically to develop and display large numbers of keyword links. This creates problems for users, in this case the classic problem of information overload through too many links.

Links appear to be random and are not well labelled; in other words, users are unsure where a link will take them or whether following the link will be useful. Links to dictionaries or glossaries produced from keywords can be more intuitive and useful, but even here the response was equivocal. Dictionaries are often assumed to be low-level texts, useful for novices and students. One way forward, instead of using ready keywords, is to look again at texts for the occurrence of what might be called link words, quite a different concept from keywords and which are created with a better understanding of the linking strategy. With new demands being placed on e-journals, perhaps link words will become an editorial task as common as creating keywords today.

On a smaller scale, it would be possible to use this technique effectively within single journals, where the effect of keyword linking would be to overlay the journal index as links on the electronic text archive. PDF linking is different again, concerned with the technical issue of managing data in a particular format rather than the content of that data. Of course, the content could be a citation link or a keyword link. Most electronic journals are in PDF so it was natural for the project to treat this as an important linking issue. Although Adobe designed PDF to include links, links are not a primary feature of the format as they are within HTML, and it is notable that few PDF journals have links.

Among the few that have citation links; some such as the American Physical Society and the Institute of Physics in the UK have reformatted reference data into HTML for the purpose. There may be good reason for this. PDF may be chosen for ease of conversion from print sources, but once in that form the data is complex and difficult to manipulate in the way required by the project's approach to linking on a large-scale, an approach which is more sophisticated than linking supported intrinsically by the format.

It required a major effort, but the project produced a working service for linking from PDF. It remains to be seen whether the dominance of PDF prevails for e-journals, but since it is more cost-effective to work with given formats rather than convert then PDF linking could be an important tool. Although converting references to HTML is one alternative, it does not address the need for links, keyword links perhaps when the implementation is refined, within the body of papers. There is, however, the danger that the PDF tools will have to be updated every time there is a change to the linking framework, as happened during the project, or each time Adobe changes the specification for PDF or the way in which it supports the format. In principle; because Open Journal linking is a server-side process, this approach is both independent of the platform used and of the version of a given software application on the user's machine.

Adobe PDF may be a de facto standard as far as e-journals are concerned, but it is still a proprietary format, and this is not ideal in an environment such as the Web which promotes the use of open, public standards that are intended to allow improved interoperability between applications. User responses were gathered by the project in a number of ways: meetings with individual users, selected evaluation groups, and open access demonstrators, mediated by electronic mail and Web forms; and less directly through meetings with other interested groups, conference presentations, seminars, and workshops.

The Web as a whole is one example. Citation linking will be another case in point. With the exception of Acrobat it seems the practice of software download does not apply to typical e-journal users, as the project soon discovered from publishers and librarians. So the link service software was rewritten to work at the server end, mediated by a user-set browser proxy. Even this was insufficient. Libraries do not want settings on shared machines to be altered, and proxy settings can interfere with firewalls in corporate environments.

In the latest version the direction to the proxy server is attached to the URL, leaving the user to browse the Web conventionally and do nothing to receive the link service, barring starting from the right place! The interface is the user's starting point, and Web interface design has advanced enormously in the last year or two, especially for large resources, where so-called "gateways" have leapt in importance.

The number of online journals is growing dramatically is becoming something of a cliché, but not everything is changing so fast. As established publishers bring existing journals to the World Wide Web we are witnessing not so much an evolution but, in many cases, direct replication, even down to the actual appearance of the original printed page when it is viewed online. If the journal article is the basic building block of the scholarly literature, then the journals are the walls. By leaving these walls in exactly the same arrangement as in the print environment, however, the limitations of which are becoming increasingly apparent, the online user is just as enclosed in his or her subject domain, within his or her library, as before.

Simply, this is not sustainable. By embracing the Web, as journal publishers are, the assumption must be that everything, not just certain things, will change. This includes the structure of journals publishing and the journals themselves, even down to the form of individual articles and the ways and styles in which they are authored. The most fundamental problem facing journal readers, library users and, it follows, librarians, is physically to get hold of all the journal articles they need when they need them.

Experience varies enormously of course, but the days in which every essential journal was held in all major academic libraries have passed. The reason most commonly cited is economic, that journal price inflation has outstripped library (and personal subscriber) budgets, with rationalisation the inevitable result. There has also been growth in the number of journal titles, which reflects changes within traditional academic disciplines: broadening and subsequent fragmentation within fields, and greater emphasis on cross-disciplinary work. With the emergence of the Web, conventional, largely failing, print-world responses to these issues may no longer be relevant.

Cutting through this complexity, some points stand out. Rightly or wrongly, the dominant motivation for scholarly journals publishing today, whether by commercial publishers, learned societies or university presses, is profitability. Commercial publishing exists to serve markets, so users, librarians too, have an influence. The above suggests that journals markets are not being served, however. While the long-running arguments over journal prices, the so-called 'serials crisis', have failed to resolve this problem, indeed have exacerbated it, the likelihood is that this issue of access will be a turning point. It affects most users more directly than do journal prices.

The critical new factor is the Web, a massively popular platform that not only offers the chance to prevent further deterioration, but to transform access to the literature. The technology of the Web can be used for different purposes to suit different users in different disciplines, but as soon as that new functionality is fully realised so the purpose of journals publishing in all disciplines will also, ultimately, be transformed. In principle academic research is progressive, one of its central tenets being that work should not be unnecessarily duplicated.

Although not referring specifically to scholarly works, Barlow adds a new perspective: 'Information that isn't moving ceases to exist as anything but potential ... at least until it is allowed to move again.' For a scholarly work, what characterises 'moving' is its ability to influence other work, that is, to be read, commented, acted upon or referenced by others in the field. While it can never be guaranteed that a work will be acted on or responded to, its influence will certainly be seriously proscribed if reader access to the publishing journals is difficult. Networked electronic, or online, publishing represents a profound change from existing practice that has become commonly delineated in this way as a switch from static (print) to dynamic or 'moving' (online) information.

Okerson anticipated the significance: '... the moment information becomes mobile, rather than static, this transformation fundamentally alters the way in which information is used, shared, and eventually created.' This is not universally accepted. Peek and Barron, for example, are more cautious about claims for technological change and its impact, but in this case the evidence for sustainable change-current experience and the widespread acceptance of the Web-is compelling. There are persuasive historical visions.

The revelation of the Web, to commercial publishers at least, is that they can no longer be sure what has value, or what people are prepared to pay for. The volume of material freely available on the Web, and its improving quality in parts, suggests that it is not textual content that obtains financial value automatically as it does in print. Instead, it is widely suggested, services are the key. According to a European Commission study on electronic publishing developments, 'electronic publishers must focus on integrating their content with services, customer-driven product tailoring (and) the brokering of information.'

When print articles and journal issues were simply discrete entities, libraries and secondary publishers provided some integration through services such as bibliographic cataloguing, indexing and abstracting. The introduction of

Web-based library catalogues will begin to speed up access to individual journal articles where electronic versions are available, but there are still many problems. Critics such as Dempsey have highlighted the gap in providing detail about journal articles actually held by an individual library. On the other hand, digital libraries such as the Perseus Project have shown that a critical mass of multimedia, multivalent materials can be a catalyst for the transformation of practice.

Indirectly, there is evidence that users are ready to accept dramatic changes in practice. A major stimulus for improved access to electronic articles is increased electronic collaboration between researchers. Wulf defined this environment as the 'collaboratory', merging 'collaboration' and 'laboratory' to describe a '.. center without walls, in which researchers can perform their research without regard to geographical location-interacting with colleagues, accessing instrumentation, sharing data and computational resource, and accessing information in digital libraries.'

The recently completed Distributed, Collaboratory Experiment Environments (DCEE) in the USA involved seven testbed projects representing scientific environments of various scales and involving from tens to hundreds of scientists and students. Search engines are widely used on the Web, and increasing use is being made of custom alerting services to bring newly published material to attention promptly. To these means of integration must be added the hypertext link. The link is the single most important, characteristic feature of Web pages. Just as it is rare to find links in online journal papers, especially those reproduced from a print original, so too citations were absent from the earliest journals.

Given that citations are an integral feature of the modern scholarly paper, it is not hard to anticipate how citation links will proliferate in Web-based journals. The likely effect of citation linking can be gauged by recognising a direct parallel with citation indexing, which is sometimes referred to as 'forward' referencing (i.e. for a given article, all the subsequent papers that cite it), developed by Garfield. Citation linking combines the two approaches, mapping both reference data and citation index data on to the text in the form of links.

Adding electronic links to the literature is introducing a new culture in many respects, but citation linking is likely to be acceptable to the academic community because it builds on practices established in other forms such as print. Further, citation linking between journal articles will only be effective if links are direct to the referenced article, and this immediately presents difficulties, not just technical difficulties, but the need to pass through commercial walls, between other journals or other publishers, that are a legacy of print journals.

New applications are highlighting this problem, but interim solutions are emerging. Another example, Physical Review Online Archives (PROLA) posts two lists on each document information page: the first provides a link to all PROLA articles that are referenced by the current article, and the second lists links to all the later papers that reference the current paper, including any errata that may have appeared. 'This hyperlinked cross-reference system allows users to locate and traverse a thread of related articles.' PROLA offers hyperlinks to articles within the PROLA system, will automatically locate and list all references to archived articles from the 1996 online APS journals, and there are plans to offer links to other, non-APS, online journals that reference

Physical Review. Institute of Physics Publishing (IoPP) in the UK was one of the first journal publishers to make all of its titles available online.

Its latest development is the Hypercite Project, through which a subscriber can link from a reference in any online IoPP paper to an abstract (if it exists) from an Inspec-provided database or can link directly to the full-text article within another IoPP journal. Online versions of IoPP journals can be purchased as a site licence on terms, in the UK at least, which encourage purchase of the whole journals catalogue, thereby making it possible to link between full-text papers within IoPP's site.

The wider world of full-text physics papers beyond IoPP is mimicked by substituting the abstracts service. For users, even this should prove to be a significant step forward. Similarly, Electronic Press, through its BioMedNet service for scientists in biology and medicine, links citations to full-text articles in journals it owns, and other citations are linked to abstracts in its Evaluated Medline database. Broadly, the project, funded by the UK Electronic Libraries (eLib) programme, addresses the issue of information coherence in the information environment currently served by academic libraries.

An increasing proportion of the diverse information assets in this environment are becoming electronic, and from a single 'terminal' users can access journals, databases and articles but, as we have seen, are required to navigate a complicated path through many providers' information gateways to locate any particular piece of information. The goal of the project is to develop a framework of information retrieval technologies (based around the DLS) and to establish electronic publishing practices to be used by information providers (especially journal publishers, but also by librarians, perhaps) which will allow them to make publications available not as isolated resources, but as cooperating assets within an information delivery environment: the 'open' journal. The facilities of the DLS, which allow authors to create links between arbitrary Web documents and then to publish those links for the benefit of other users, provide a basis for reintegrating the online literature.

In hypertext terms, they allow authors to turn a bounded subset of the Web from a hyperbase, an undistinguished database of information nodes, into a hyperdocument, a collection of documents united by authorial intent. One of the major features of the DLS is that, instead of inserting link data within the html (or other) coding of a source document, the data are held separately in a link database, or linkbase. The links can be viewed superimposed on a Web page, as though a transparency were overlaid on it, by retrieving the document from a url via a proxy link server. This is easily set up using the standard menu facilities on popular Web browsers. The links appear to act as conventional Web links, so the application of the link service is effectively transparent, while at the same time it provides the link author and user with significantly improved link flexibility.

It is this capability of separating links from the authored content which is perhaps the key to allowing journals to interoperate, because it allows the creation of links between two third-party resources, not just to another publisher's documents, but from them as well. Imagine an institutional library has introduced a new rule governing the use of its books and journals. To be allowed to take out a book, users need to present the issue desk not with the book itself, but some other book which contains a citation for the book actually required. Only when the librarian sees a valid citation for a book or journal will the user be allowed to read it. Further, the staff choose to keep all books behind the counter, inaccessible to library users but directly available to qualified librarians. In this scenario there is no way to idly look through stacks of new periodicals to keep abreast of the latest developments, nor can users select the particular book required on a topic by inspecting the whole range of books available on that topic.

This is almost the situation that users of the Web find themselves in, an environment where a private collection of documents can be requested individually, but only given a valid reference to the document. In both situations, neither the identity of a document, nor even its existence, can be deduced or guessed. Much activity has been directed at the former-producing lists of content, and lists of lists, making catalogues and indexes of subject material on the Web-but less in authoring and publishing links, towards which the link service is directed.

One likely effect of using a link service in a professional publishing environment, such as journals publishing, will be to transform link authoring into a link publishing task, possibly handled by link editors. In this way links are added at the moment of publication rather than during the authoring stage, an important feature in a dynamically changing environment such as the Web. The link maintenance problem also becomes more manageable. In addition the Open Journal project has extended the core functions of the DLS to work not just with html documents but also portable document formats viewed with Adobe Acrobat. To demonstrate the concept the project is producing three Open Journals in the areas of biology, cognitive science and computer science.

Each consists of original journals from a number of different primary and secondary publishers, served from a number of different sites in a number of data formats (principally html and pdf). Dictated by differing cultures, academic disciplines show various degrees of acceptance of online publishing, adopting different approaches. This is borne out by clear distinctions between the three Open Journals.

Biologists have access to a diverse range of online materials, from journals to books, databases of gene sequences and other molecular structures, libraries of graphical images and teaching resources. The information is invariably well catalogued and often freely accessible. The databases in particular form a focal point for the field, lending it an online coherence that few other disciplines can match and attracting a higher proportion of the field's prestigious journals online than other fields.

This area also provides the project with its longest list of participating journals, one of the project objectives in this case to begin to link these journals into the non-journal data resources. In contrast, computer science offers large volumes of disparate online resources with little organisation apart from some loosely catalogued indexes, although there is an attempt to build a coherent 'library' of networked computer science technical reports. Few established computer science journals are available online, and the odd new online journals in this field, with one or two exceptions, have been noticeably slow to grow.

The DLS can be used to overcome the lack of links on most Web journals by dynamically matching a fixed database of pre-defined links against the contents of an article, inserting a link whenever an explicit match occurs. More general than a programming language GOTO statement, a link is the specification of a relationship between a data source and destination where both the source and destination may expand to one of several places in a particular set of documents.

These flexible relationships are usually coded explicitly by the DLS as a generic link, but they may be the by-product of a more complicated processing arrangement. For the purpose of citation linking this involves matching citations and bibliography lists in a document against a database of bibliographic information. This is a complex process which requires an understanding of the house style of the publication, an understanding of the document coding format and the ability to parse complex language structures. Since this is a knowledge-based activity being undertaken on behalf of the user, we call it a citation agent.

When the DLS processes a document which is defined to be in the Cognitive Science Open Journal, it launches the agent to act on the document before adding other links in the usual way. In short, with the arrival and, in some fields, broad acceptance of a core mass of scholarly online journals, the most progressive of these journals are evidently heading towards a new phase in which they are being enhanced to take advantage of the capabilities of the Web.

Tools to support this new functionality are proliferating. Among them, link services offer the potential to transform the use of the dominating feature of the Web, the hypertext link. Distributed link service (DLS) is a new service which can be used to provide hypermedia links for users of information environments, in particular the World Wide Web. In the same way that a client connects to a remote Web server to access a document, DLS allows the client to connect to a link server to request a set of links to apply to the data in a document.

From an abstract viewpoint it provides a hypermedia link service which can be used alongside, but separately from, the WWW's document data service: in practice the link service is mediated by the WWW, and implemented by CGI processes located on Web servers. The WWW has a well-established method for expressing links as attributes of its native document format, and so the link service will provide a complementary set of links on top of those standard facilities. By contrast, a simple text editor has no built-in hypertext links, and so the link service provides an otherwise non-existent service to such users.

Without a link service, Web users can follow links from HTML documents or 'imagemapped' pictures into dead-end media such as spreadsheets, CAD documents or text; with the link service they can also follow links out of these media again. A link service can provide several practical benefits to information systems: it can act as an adjunct to provide hypermedia facilities for applications without requiring a rewrite of the applications themselves, and, by allowing links to be manipulated as independent objects can aid in the document maintenance effort since a document does no longer needs to be revised in order to change its links.

In fact, a document does not even need to be revisable; links may be applied to legacy documents or data stored on read-only media, and the relationship of a document to the larger docuverse may evolve over time, even though the document itself remains static. These flexible relationships can be expressed in a simple way, and stored together in database; the link service is effectively a database lookup service where the data items are interpreted as links between other data items.

It allows for both HTML-style links, where the link is coded in situ at one of its end points, and also for independent links, where the link is coded in a section or document separate from the data which it links together. Although the DLS does not yet use the HyTime standard coding, it uses the HyTime concepts of links as independent entities. The links themselves are distributed across a number of databases and the databases can be distributed across a number of servers.

Further, the document server may provide only a basic set of link databases, whereas the end user may have a private set of link databases and a third party server may provide some sets of specialist links on a commercial basis. Given the existence of this link service, there are a number of different ways that it can be used to achieve benefit for different groups of users.

For an information consumer on the Web, the link service provides an additional means of navigation that can be tailored very precisely to his or her exact needs. When the user wishes to investigate links from some information, they select the data of interest and choose the Follow Link menu item from the interface agent. The agent grabs the current selection, tries to determine the current document context, parcels this information into a message which is sent to the link server. This process consists of creating an HTTP message with POST data and sending it to a Web server, since the link service is actually hosted by the Web. The link server then responds with a set of links which are available from the specified selection in the specified document.

In some respects this process is similar to making an enquiry of a Virtual Library—certainly the same kind of database lookup is going on, and a similar-looking page of HTML is returned. On the other hand, this activity is both document centered, occurring while the user's focus is on the information content instead of the navigation superstructure, and context specific, parameterised by the location of the query data. If this action is not totally like a database query, it is also not completely like a normal link following operation. It is reader-driven rather than author driven as it is the user who decides what is of interest for link following rather than the author's sole perogative to determine what material can be followed up.

In fact one kind of hypertext can be implemented using just such a text retrieval service, where the links are all derived by a statistical analysis of the lexical data contained in the documents. This style of hypertext, known as a hyperbase, is characterised by the lack of internal structure as opposed to a hyperdocument in which the links are created by human authorship. Services like WAIS and the Virtual Libraries provide some similar features to the DLS, but lack the capability to express human-authored links.

The DLS on the other hand can implement a range of links, from the human authored variety through to the automatic keyword matching variety. Another feature of the DLS is that it allows link following to be affected not just by the static document context of the link source, but also the reader's dynamic context: task-specific information that affects the kind of resources that they would like to follow up. Authors may make use of the DLS by using the same interface agent.

Since a part of the authoring process involves the author taking on the role of a reader, the author can benefit from the link service exactly as a reader can, but in addition an author can create links and edit link databases. To create a link, the author highlights the link source, chooses Start Link from the interface agent, finds the link destination, highlights it and chooses End Link. At this stage the interface agent packs the selections, static document context and dynamic user context information into a Create Link message and sends it to the link server via the Web.

The newly-created link may be added to the user's personal link database or to the current Context database; either of these may be subsequently edited by a forms-based interface in the Web browser. This kind of functionality is fairly straight-forward, but the real advantage for the author comes in the kinds of link definition that are allowed. Following the Microcosm model, upon which much of this work is based, links may be declared to be more or less generic, i.e. having the location of the selected text constrained to appear more or less specifically within the static document context. A standard link applies only at the exact place that the link source was selected, whereas a completely generic link will match the link source's selection at any place in any document.

One of the major benefits of this authoring style is the scope for information reuse: not only can the author vary the internal paths through the documents by changing the link databases, but also the documents themselves can be used and reused in many different situations by providing different sets of 'into' and 'out of' links. Link databases use an SGML-based format, and so can be processed using standard tools like Perl, sed or awk. In particular it is possible for an author to automatically create a simple link database from scratch by extracting sets of keywords from documents and turning them into generic links.

Access to the network will allow every citizen to communicate interactively between libraries, with museums, galleries and the media, with local and national government, with public services, and with agencies in the voluntary and private sectors. Moreover, there will also be the capability for communication within and between communities, whether they be local or global, founded on geography or on a common purpose.

Public libraries are already used by 58 per cent of the population. They are a first stop for information, they are widely used by children and young people as an adjunct to formal learning, and their reputation for supporting the knowledge-seeker is unparalleled. Their unique combination of resources, services and personal support attracts some 1.3 million visitors every working day, and 10 million users visit frequently - at least once a fortnight. Library staff respond to over 50 million enquiries each year, on a universal range of topics.

In the information society, making information and communication networks accessible to every citizen will be vital to generate the energy for success. The new and growing range of resources and facilities which networking can deliver, combined with the existing assets of the public library system, will form the core of a powerhouse of knowledge, enabling the smallest and most isolated local library to offer the same range, depth and quality of information as a large centra central library, providing equal access to the global and the local. Public libraries complement formal education provision by providing a resource base and a platform for people of all ages to participate in lifelong learning.

Rich multimedia resources provided after school, in a safe, culturally creative environment, will help overcome the inequality of opportunity experienced by those who do not have access to new technology at home. Several studies have indicated that children can benefit both educationally and socially from having well-managed access to various forms of information and communication technology (ICT) from an early age.

The early introduction to independent learning in the library will promote a more rounded education, while also imparting the skills needed to learn independently in later years. Knowledge is power - and universal access to information is a hallmark of freedom in a democracy but knowledge is also discovery, excitement, personal growth and self-confidence. The use of existing services demonstrates that there is no limit to the type of information which people seek every day in libraries. Digital communications in the information society will bring new resources in unprecedented quantity, making available the equivalent of millions of pages of words and pictures.

The library as an entry point to the information superhighway will bring unprecedented opportunities to learn for leisure, to find out for fun, and to experience the personal fulfilment of discovery. Through the networked public library, existing library resources will be newly opened up to more people. The catalogues of public library collections currently accessible only locally will be linked to create a UK-wide library system. This rich collective resource will be available at any local library. Eventually, catalogues will be enhanced with requesting systems so that remote users can locate and order the items they need.

Cross-sectoral access (public/FE/HE) will introduce the flexibility of access to resources inherent in the concepts of open and distance learning. Such a wealth of resources will make digital discovery an awesome and exciting experience, but many people will need the support of a trusted and accountable intermediary - not only in accessing but also in interpreting and evaluating what is available.

With library staff providing this support, the unique role of the library as 'the people's university' will be immeasurably enhanced. The accessibility of public libraries, enhanced by networking technologies, will ensure that people with mobility problems will find it easy to exploit the new opportunities. At the same time, as systems develop on the back of current research, services will be adapted for use by people with impaired sight or hearing.

People with disabilities have the same desires to find out and learn as others: the information society must not be one in which they experience exclusion. The UK Public Library Network will also be a gateway for citizen communications - an opening to the networked society which will promote a healthy democracy and social cohesion. In recent times disillusion with political, legal and social institutions has generated an atmosphere of cynicism and alienation.

People - particularly young people - have distanced themselves from a system which they see as irrelevant to their circumstances. A public library network of access points, open to every citizen, for the delivery of information on government and government services - both local and UK-wide - and, especially, for enabling interactive communications with government and others, will help bring a sense of belonging and renew the potential for participation in society. Such a network will stimulate the production of digital information and interactive services for citizens which has already been explored by some government departments and local authorities.

Many public agencies now have Internet Web sites; these will be further developed to meet the increased expectation of citizens using the library network. Easier two-way transfer of information and documentation between people and providers will also allow faster and more efficient routine transactions with government and public services, leaving more time for citizen and public servant to interact face to face on individual issues of greater sensitivity. A healthy society must also communicate with itself, and the UK Public Library Network will not only provide access to the centres of administration but will enable people to interact with all manner of voluntary organisations and interest groups.

Individuals will be able to become better informed and to promote their views in the interests of wider community development. When citizens are openly and freely in communication with government, democracy can be said to have 'grown up'. Those groups generally regarded as 'minorities' are, together, the majority; ensuring improved access for those with a minority or special interest will also enhance the quality of life for the whole of society. The successful business already exploits information as an organisational resource.

However, the majority of businesses in the UK are small and medium-sized enterprises - around 73 per cent of companies employ fewer than ten people - and such companies, and the 3 million self-employed, do not have the capacity to employ information specialists or to acquire expensive collections of data to inform their marketing and development activities. Public libraries - especially the major city libraries - have variously developed enormous print-based resources to support business; the UK Public Library Network will allow still larger amounts of information to be available to even the smallest and most remote local library through access to remote databases on trade and commerce.

The technology will allow greater cooperation to inform and support the UK's industrial, commercial and financial enterprise. The library has always been a resource for learning, and has a specially important role to play in learning in order to update or acquire job skills. Citizens are also consumers, and thus the ultimate generators of national wealth. The consumer needs ready and reliable access to information on products, services and producers, as well as access to legal and commercial information - all of which the UK Public Library Network will provide.

The IT for All initiative aims to raise awareness of ICT, provide access, and develop the ICT skills of individual citizens, and specifically adults. Inherent within the capability of networking technologies is the capacity to reconstitute the visual into the virtual and to deliver it from its custodial home to the widest community in local libraries - and indeed elsewhere. The significant collections in public libraries - photographs, rare books, maps - as well as their sister collections in museums and galleries, will be converted to create online collections which are accessible not only to researchers but to all citizens, supporting cultural awareness and identity. More imaginatively, multimedia exhibitions - images, narrative, background - which can be visited on-screen in local libraries will give everyone the opportunity for the 'guided tour' as opposed to the 'passive walkabout'.

In addition to the value of giving the tax-payer greater direct access to publicly funded collections, such technology will also allow the development of new approaches to the visual arts and their promotion; projected through networks to an international audience, this will create the ultimate marketing tool in promoting the UK's cultural heritage to the peoples of the world. This will foster and support the tourism industry. Public libraries have already demonstrated their capacity to guide beginners in using information and communication technologies and to help individuals develop their 'computeracy'. Integral to public library networking will be provision for training/learning in the new technology.

At an introductory level this may be provided by library staff, who will encounter the uninitiated on a daily basis, but learning organisations and private companies will be enthusiastic to collaborate with library service providers in developing strategies for public training/learning provision. As trusted intermediaries, public libraries can span the present and the technological future, ensuring no citizen is left behind, providing a safety net against alienation and social exclusion from technological advance - a route to universal access and opportunity.

Networking public libraries will take the UK's public library system through a period of substantial change into the new era of the information society. During the transition years, and for the foreseeable future in some areas, the demand for books and other non-networked resources will continue; meanwhile a UK-wide lead and financial support will be necessary to generate the range of electronic resources and services which users will expect of their networked local library.

The range of resources and services envisaged will depend on a UK-wide initiative involving unprecedented collaboration, planning and investment, and we recommend that an agency be established to direct and manage the development process. In UK, the National Digital Library envisaged in the plan will depend on the conversion of special and rare collections into digital format. A major project to identify and prioritise appropriate collections of items will be needed; it should look across all sectors to locate opportunities for partnership with collections in museums, galleries and the national libraries. A range of services will exist to allow library users to discover both free and commercial resources on the Internet. It is important that all development work proceeds within a common framework of information standards and best practice.

The public library is an important focal point in the community. There is a feeling that its position has been eroded, that it does not currently present a compelling reason to go there and that it is lagging behind the times rather than moving ahead. Though there is a tremendous amount of goodwill for the public library service among users, there is a significant opportunity to revitalise libraries, stimulate greater usage, broaden the appeal, and make a big difference in people's lives. New technology and networked libraries are essential if libraries are to gain status in the new world of networked information, knowledge and learning.

IT could be a big step forward in encouraging learning - making it seem more fun and motivating, especially to those who currently feel that libraries are not for them. People really value the quiet learning space provided by the library at the moment, and any development needs to be complementary to this. There were some indications from our research that new uses would add value to the library in an exciting way, but that they would require separate spaces. The future of librarians will be to enable and facilitate.

The overall purpose of the job will be essentially the same, but the skills needed will be different. Librarians will have to think about their role, management skills, delivering services and 'customer care', and this may require a cultural shift in attitude for some. More librarians have to come out from behind the desk and be more outward-going.

The development of IT in public libraries was regarded as essential if libraries are to play an integral role in the new world of networked information, knowledge and learning. Respondents were impressed by what the information technology network could potentially deliver, and a large majority reacted very favourably. The most enthusiastic were the better informed - aware of the Internet capabilities, and conscious of the fact that, if libraries did not go ahead with public library networking and be part of the global network, they would get left behind.

The applications of networking libraries that aroused most enthusiasm tended to concern education and support for lifelong learning, while levelling the playing-field for those unlikely to be able to afford to buy the new technology themselves. People perceived the library as the natural place for self-learning and training in appropriate skills. The librarian was seen to have an important role to play in helping and coaching people in IT.

The presence of the librarian was also necessary to maintain a 'human feel' - especially to encourage those people with 'techno-fear', worried about the 'coldness' and inaccessibility of IT. The library was regarded as a good place to go to pursue self-education with more personal goals, or leisure interests and hobbies. Primarily it provided a quiet study space and reference materials that people could use in their own time - provided the library was open. The majority thought that IT skills were necessary in a world in which technology-based employment is growing, and some had already taken steps to acquire these skills through public libraries. The concept of open learning in a library environment was appealing to many, though a minority felt they would personally prefer to have the greater social interaction from attending a course.

The greatest barrier for some would initially be that they would need to acquire basic computer skills and to overcome some kind of 'techno-fear' in order to do this. A few more socially minded females recognised the value in encouraging literacy among people disadvantaged by a culture/language who they felt would be less likely to enrol into formal education. Basic computer skills training was particularly appealing, though it seemed more appropriate for adults than for younger groups, who were already taught such skills at school. The idea of an introductory session to the Internet created strong interest in all groups.

Centres where people could improve interpersonal communication skills generated interest and appeal across all groups, and overall the library was felt to be an appropriate place to house them. The opportunities presented by videoconference links had broad appeal. As well as education-related use, the most relevant general application was as a way to access support groups in health matters. The relevance of the subject-matter would encourage people to use unfamiliar technology and to acquire basic skills. The idea of shared learning experiences through this channel had mixed appeal.

The prospect of being able to 'attend' a lecture or consult an expert remotely was very motivating for a few, though the majority of the people we talked to were uninterested in this possibility. Learning a language was of interest to a few, as was the benefit of being able to have a tutorial if doing a correspondence course. Access to advanced services, such as virtual reality, was especially motivating for younger male audiences, who were very enthusiastic at the prospect and thought it appropriate as long as the ideas were information- or communication-related.

It was seen as a way for the library to move ahead and provide a unique service in allowing people to try out and use the latest new technology. People were passionate about books, about being surrounded by books in peace and quiet, able to browse and find the unexpected - all important library values people do not want to lose. There was a general consensus that initial trial of IT services, and basic instruction, should be free.

In the past, reference service has involved on-site service and local telephone support, designed to instruct and assist library users in their research endeavours. Now, digital reference is becoming an important remote service, as ever growing numbers of library users are learning and researching at a distance. The short definition of digital reference is the provision of reference service over the Internet.

The term for digital reference has taken many forms: digital, virtual, chat, on-line and real-time, to mention a few of the more popular names. More recently, distributed reference services, captures best the notion that the modern day library, to a great degree, is a web-based learning environment. The lines between on and off-campus students and courses are blurring as technology is incorporated into all aspects of education.

Digital reference differs from traditional reference in two fundamental ways. First, there is a disconnect between the user and the physical space of the library. Second, digital reference creates artifacts of the exchange between librarian and user. That is, the transaction can be recorded in terms of the content of the interaction, the resources used, the time it took, the time of day it took place, the librarian involved, the general location of the user and a number of other quantifiable variables. On many library Web sites, the user is hard-pressed to identify the staff, whose names, if they're there, are five levels down. The human factor is still important.

In addition to email reference, the Library offers online library research tutorials, web-based subject guides, an FAQ page, and a telephone call centre. The launch of the Library's chat-based reference service, Ask a Librarian Live, gave us the opportunity to revamp our Ask a Librarian page with the help of the Digital Media Projects Office (DMP). After some deliberation and exploration, the Library decided on acquiring software that provided the highest level of interaction with our users and resources.

The buzz in the digital reference world is about providing "high tech with high touch." The software acquired is in fact not considered chat but web call centre software and it differs from chat platforms in a number of ways. The most significant difference is the ability to co-browse web pages while conversing (chatting) via text with the user. The librarians considered this feature important because it gives the ability to assist users "inside" licensed databases.

5

Archiving and Preserving Challenges

Digital technology, poses new threats and problems as well as new opportunities. Its functionality comes with complexity. Anyone with a compass (or a clear night to view the position of the stars in relation to true north) could theoretically set up or repair a sundial. A digital watch is more useful and accurate for telling time than a sundial, but few people can repair it or even understand how it works. Reading and understanding information in digital form requires equipment and software, which is changing constantly and may not be available within a decade of its introduction. Even newer technology such as 9-track tape is rapidly becoming obsolete. Rapid changes in the means of recording information, in the formats for storage, and in the technologies for use threaten to render the life of information in the digital age as, to borrow a phrase from Hobbes, "nasty, brutish and short."

Some information no doubt deserves such a fate, but numerous examples illustrate the danger of losing valuable cultural memories that may appear in digital form. In 1976, the US, National Archives identified seven series of aggregated data from the 1960 Census files as having long-term historical value. A large portion of the selected records, however, resided on tapes that the Bureau could read only with a UNIVAC type II-A tape drive. By the mid-seventies, that particular tape drive was long obsolete, and the Census Bureau faced a significant engineering challenge in preserving the data from the UNIVAC type II-A tapes.

By 1979, the Bureau had successfully copied onto industry-standard tapes nearly all the data judged then to have long-term value. Though largely successful in the end, the data rescue effort was a signal event that helped move the Committee on the Records of Government six years later to proclaim that "the United States is in danger of losing its memory." The Committee did not bother to describe the actual details of the migration of the 1960 census records. Nor did it analyze the effects on the integrity of the constitutionally-mandated census of the nearly 10,000 records of aggregated data that the rescue effort did not successfully recover.

Instead, it chose to register its warning on the dangers of machine obsolescence in apocryphal terms. With more than a little hyperbole, it wrote that "when the computer tapes containing the raw data from the 1960 federal census came to the attention of NARS [the National Archives and Records Service], there were only two machines in the world capable of reading those tapes: one in Japan and the other already deposited in the Smithsonian as a relic". Other examples lack the memorable but false details accompanying the 1960 Census story, but they do equally illustrate how readily we can lose our heritage in electronic form when the custodian makes no plans for long-term retention in a changing technical environment. In 1964, the first electronic mail message was sent from either the Massachusetts Institute of Technology, the Carnegie Institute of Technology or Cambridge University.

The message does not survive, however, and so there is no documentary record to determine which group sent the pathbreaking message. Satellite observations of Brazil in the 1970s, critical for establishing a time-line of changes in the Amazon basin, are also lost on the now obsolete tapes to which they were written. Similarly, in the late 1960s, the New York State Department of Commerce and Cornell University undertook the Land Use and Natural Resources Inventory Project (LUNR).

The LUNR project produced a computerized map of New York State depicting patterns of land usage and identifying natural resources. It created a primitive geographic information system by superimposing a matrix over aerial photographs of the entire state and coding each cell according to its predominant features. The data were used for several comprehensive studies of land use patterns that informed urban planning, economic development, and environmental policy. In the mid-1980s, the New York State Archives obtained copies of the tapes containing the data from the LUNR inventory along with the original aerial photographs and several thousand mylar transparencies. Staff at the State Archives attempted to preserve the LUNR tapes, but the problems proved insurmountable.

The LUNR project had depended on customized software programs to represent and analyze the data, and these programs were not saved with the data. Even if the software had been retained, the hardware and operating system needed to run the software were no longer available. As a consequence, researchers wishing to study changes in land use patterns now have to re-digitize the data from the hard-copy base maps and transparencies at the State Archives or rekey data from printouts at Cornell's Department of Manuscripts & University Archives.

Today, information technologies that are increasingly powerful and easy to use, especially like those that support the World Wide Web, have unleashed the production and distribution of digital information. Such information is penetrating and transforming nearly every aspect of our culture. If we are effectively to preserve for future generations the portion of this rapidly expanding corpus of information in digital form that represents our cultural record, we need to understand the costs of doing so and we need to commit ourselves technically, legally, economically and organizationally to the full dimensions of the task.

Failure to look for trusted means and methods of digital preservation will certainly exact a stiff, long-term cultural penalty. Archivists responsible for governmental and corporate records have been acutely aware of the difficulties entailed in trying to ensure that digital information survives for future generations. Far more than their library colleagues, who have continued to collect and organize published materials primarily in paper form, archivists have observed the materials for which they are responsible shift rapidly from paper objects produced on typewriters and other analog devices to include files created in word processor, spreadsheet and many other digital forms.

Early attention to the difficulties in preserving digital information focused on the longevity of the physical media on which the information is stored. Even under the best storage conditions, however, digital media can be fragile and have limited shelf life. Moreover, new devices, processes and software are replacing the products and methods used to record, store, and retrieve digital information on breathtaking cycles of 2- to 5- years. Given such rates of technological change, even the most fragile media may well outlive the continued availability of readers for those media.

Efforts to preserve physical media thus provide only a short-term, partial solution to the general problem of preserving digital information. Indeed, technological obsolescence represents a far greater threat to information in digital form than the inherent physical fragility of many digital media. In the face of rapid technological obsolescence and to overcome the problem of media fragility, archivists have adopted the technique of "refreshing" digital information by copying it onto new media.

Copying from medium to medium, however, also suffers limitations as a means of digital preservation. Refreshing digital information by copying will work as an effective preservation technique only as long as the information is encoded in a format that is independent of the particular hardware and software needed to use it and as long as there exists software to manipulate the format in current use. Otherwise, copying depends either on the compatibility of present and past versions of software and generations of hardware or the ability of competing hardware and software product lines to interoperate. In respect of these factors-backward compatibility and interoperability-the rate of technological change exacts a serious toll on efforts to ensure the longevity of digital information.

Digital information today is produced in highly varying degrees of dependence on particular hardware and software. Moreover, it is costly and difficult for vendors to assure that their products are either "backwardly compatible" with previous versions or that they can interoperate with competing products. Refreshing digital information by copying it from medium to medium and the possibility of maintaining a complex set of emulators describe two distinct points on a continuum of approaches to preserving digital information. However, neither refreshing nor emulation sufficiently describes the full range of options needed and available for digital preservation. Instead, a better and more general concept to describe these options is migration.

Migration is the periodic transfer of digital materials from one hardware/software configuration to another, or from one generation of computer technology to a subsequent generation. The purpose of migration is to preserve the integrity of digital objects and to retain the ability for clients to retrieve, display, and otherwise use them in the face of constantly changing technology. Migration includes refreshing as a means of digital preservation but differs from it in the sense that it is not always possible to make an exact digital copy or replica of a database or other information object as hardware and software change and still maintain the compatibility of the object with the new generation of technology. Even for information that is encoded in a contemporary standard form, forward migration of the information to a new standard or application program is, as anyone knows who has witnessed or participated in such a process, time-consuming, costly and much more complex than simple refreshing.

Compounding the technical challenges of migrating digital information is the problem of managing the process in a legal and organizational environment that is in flux as it moves to accommodate rapidly changing digital technologies. Consider, for example, the barriers to decisive preservation action caused by widespread uncertainty about legal and organizational requirements for managing the intellectual property that digital information represents.

Addressing and resolving the legal and practical questions of migrating intellectual property in digital form necessarily involves a complex set of interested parties, including the creators and owners of intellectual property, managers of digital archives, representatives of the public interest, and actual and potential users of intellectual property. Owners of intellectual property are unsure about how to price access to their information and worry, given the ease of copying, that the first digital copy of a work they sell may be the only copy they sell. Users of intellectual property are unsure about what rights are conveyed with the use of a particular digital information object and about how much such use is worth.

Government representatives seek in the public interest to manage the powerful changes that accompany digital technologies, but are unsure about what levels of influece are available to them and how to generate appropriate public policy. The state of the copyright law, which was generated and developed in an analog world but is applied in an increasingly digital universe, is itself confusing and uncertain. And all of these concerns are exacerbated by the fact that bits know no borders. The costs and the technical, legal and organizational complexities of moving digital information forward into the future raise our greatest fear about the life of information in the digital future: namely, that owners or custodians who can no longer bear the expense and difficulty will deliberately or inadvertently, through a simple failure to act, destroy the objects without regard for future use. Repeated anecdotes about the loss of land use information, satellite imagery or census data, even when false or misleading, feed our general anxiety about the future of the cultural record we are accumulating in digital form.

And uncertainty and lack of confidence about our will and ability to carry digital information forward into the future exert a major inhibiting force in our disposition to fully exploit the digital medium to generate, publish and disseminate information. Viewed developmentally, the problem of preserving digital information for the future is not only, or even primarily, a problem of fine tuning a narrow set of technical variables. It is not a clearly defined problem like preserving the embrittled books that are self-destructing from the acid in the paper on which they were printed.

Rather, it is a grander problem of organizing ourselves over time and as a society to maneuver effectively in a digital landscape. It is a problem of building-almost from scratch-the various systematic supports, or deep infrastructure, that will enable us to tame anxieties and move our cultural records naturally and confidently into the future. For digital preservation, the organizational effort-the process of building deep infrastructure-necessarily involves multiple, interrelated factors, many of which are either unknown or poorly defined.

One of the biggest unknowns is the full impact on traditional information handling functions of distributed computing over electronic networks. The effort to meet the cultural imperative of digital preservation thus requires a complex iteration and reiteration of exploration, development and solution as the relevant factors and their interrelationships emerge and become clearer and more tractable. And the first task in the effort is not to posit answers, but to frame questions and issues in such a way as to engage the many parties already working in various ways with digital information so that they can help us understand the relevant issues and, within the context of their work, help us identify, define and incorporate solutions that contribute to the larger, common goal of preserving our cultural heritage.

Digital archives are distinct from digital libraries in the sense that digital libraries are repositories that collect and provide access to digital information, but may or may not provide for the long-term storage and access of that information. Digital libraries thus may or may not be, in functional terms, digital archives and, in fact, much of the recent work on digital libraries is notably silent on the archival issues of ensuring long-term storage and access. Conversely, digital archives necessarily embrace digital library functions to the extent that they must select, obtain, store, and provide access to digital information. Many of the functional requirements for digital archives defined thus overlap those for digital libraries.

Many traditional libraries, archives and museums, as institutions, have taken and may well continue to assume digital library and archival functions. Certified digital archives will have available to them a critical fail-safe mechanism. Such a mechanism, supported by organizational will, economic means and legal right, would enable a certified archival repository to exercise an aggressive rescue function to save digital information that it judges to be culturally significant and which is endangered in its current repository.

The current repository may be a digital library, another digital archives, or some other individual, organizational, public or private source of digital information. Without the operation of a formal certification program and a fail-safe mechanism, preservation of the nation's cultural heritage in digital form will likely be overly dependent on marketplace forces, which may value information for too short a period and without applying broader, public interest criteria. Such development is necessary for and will contribute powerfully to the overall growth of an information-based society and economy.

Information objects in digital form, like those in other forms, move through life cycles. They are created, edited, described and indexed, disseminated, acquired, used, annotated, revised, re-created, modified and retained for future use or destroyed by a complex, interwoven community of creators and other owners, disseminators, value-added services, and institutional and individual users. The digital world is still too new for us to describe fully the life cycle of the information objects that do now or will in the future reside there, but what surely unites the community of actors in their various information-based activities is their common purpose in support of the pursuit of knowledge. The pursuit of knowledge is a process in which the emergence of new knowledge builds on and reconstructs the old.

Knowledge cannot advance without consistent and reliable access to information sources, past and present. It is the archival function in the system of knowledge creation and use that serves to identify and retain important sources of information and to ensure continuing access to them. How reliable the archival process proves to be in the emerging digital environment hinges on the trustworthy operation of digital archives and on their ability to maintain the integrity of the objects they are charged to preserve. For digital objects, no less than for objects of other kinds, knowing how operationally to preserve them depends, at least in part, on being able to discriminate the essential features of what needs to be preserved.

Digital technologies increasingly serve to integrate information resources. Text, numeric data, images, voice, and video have heretofore resided in print or other analog media for storage and transmission. When they are encoded digitally, either by conversion or at the point of creation, these various kinds of resources share layers of technology-a common means of storage and transmission- that allows them to be brought together and used in both old and new ways. Multimedia and hyperlinked objects on the World Wide Web represent some of the new kinds of information and new ways of knowing in the digital realm that bring together the traditional forms of information and transform their use.

The application of computer hardware and software has also generated other new kinds of information objects, including the products of simulation, remote sensing, computer-aided design (CAD) and geographic information (GIS) systems. These objects come into being and exist as creatures of the digital environment; if nurtured well, digital technologies will certainly beget still other kinds of information objects, which we can now only anticipate. The processes of preserving digital information will vary significantly with the different kinds of objects-textual, numeric, image, video, sound, multimedia, simulation and so on-being preserved.

Whatever preservation method is applied, however, the central goal must be to preserve information integrity; that is, to define and preserve those features of an information object that distinguish it as a whole and singular work. In the digital environment, the features that determine information integrity and deserve special attention for archival purposes include the following: content, fixity, reference, provenance, and context. What digital archives are trying to preserve after all is the intellectual substance contained in information objects.

The notion of content, however, is itself a complex idea that operates at several different levels of abstraction. To preserve the integrity of objects in their charge, digital archives must decide at which level, or levels, of abstraction they are defining information content. At the lowest level of abstraction, all digital information objects consist of simple bitstreams of 0s and 1s. One can distinguish objects from one another merely by distinguishing the configuration of bits. Preserving the integrity of an information object in this sense means preserving the bit configuration that uniquely defines the object. There are various well-established techniques, such as checksums and digests, for tracking the bit-level equivalence of digital objects and ensuring that a preserved object is identical to the original.

Defining content as a collection of bits, however, is often too limited and simplistic to be useful. In the digital environment, as we have seen, ideas are typically embedded in particular formats and structures that are dependent on hardware and software technologies subject to rapid change. In addition to character set issues, digital archives must also grapple with the means of representing and preserving textual content embedded in layout and structure.

Markup systems, such as implementations of TeX and the Standard Generalized Markup Language (SGML), do exist as platform-independent mechanisms for identifying and tagging for subsequent layout and retrieval detailed structural elements of documents. The use of TeX and its variants, for example, is relatively common among scholars in some scientific disciplines such as mathematics and computer science, and the federal government and scholarly publishers are increasingly employing the SGML standard in documents that they produce and distribute electronically. Beyond these relatively specialized segments, however, word processing and desktop publishing systems still dominate the market for the creation of documents with complex structure and layout, and the software for such use typically models and stores document structure and layout in proprietary terms.

Although software may provide mechanisms for converting documents to common interchange formats, use of such mechanisms often results in the loss or inadequate rendering of content such as page structures and the layout of headers, footers and section headings. The preservation of images comprises another example of the ways in which content, defined in terms of structure and format, poses integrity problems for digital archives. Image resolution, accuracy of color representation and compression for storage all require attention, but the interaction of these structural factors tends to pit judgments about the quality of content against the need for its efficient archival storage and use.

In general, one can express the tradeoffs as follows: the higher the resolution and the richer the color register, the larger the file size and more costly the storage. The use of compression technologies further complicates the equation because the application of some algorithms to reduce space needs may involve an irreversible loss of data. The popular JPEG algorithm, for example, supports "lossy" compression, whereby the greatest degree of compression requires the maximum settings for allowable loss.

At the highest level of abstraction, digital archives define content in a way that transcends the limits of the hardware and software systems needed for reading and interpreting the bits of an information object and for rendering it for use in a specific format and structural representation; that is, they define content in terms of the knowledge or ideas the object contains. Expressed in this way, the preservation challenge for digital archives is to migrate intellectual content using standard interchange algorithms and other appropriate migration strategies so that the ideas available in the end are identical to those contained in the original object.

The measure of integrity in the preservation process thus turns, at least in part, on informed and skillful judgments about the appropriate definition of the content of an digital information object-about the extent to which content depends on its configuration of bits, on the structure and format of its representation, and on the ideas it contains-and for what purposes. The process of identifying and preserving a digital information object as a whole and singular work goes well beyond considerations of content. It also depends, for instance, on the way that the content is fixed as a discrete object.

If an object is not fixed, and the content is subject to change or withdrawal without notice, then its integrity may be compromised and its value as a cultural record would be severely diminished. Outside the digital landscape, business practices, editorial policies, and legal constraints, have created disciplines for fixing information in discrete objects. For example, business records, such as an annual report, a letter of hire or an engineering drawing for the manufacture of a new product, are fixed in the transactions for which they constitute evidence.

The acts of production and broadcast establish radio and television programs as discrete objects. And the act of publication marks a specific version or edition of a literary work. In each of these cases, it is virtually impossible to change or withdraw the cultural record that the release of an information object establishes. On the digital landscape, by contrast, it is still relatively easy for a creator to alter or retract previously released information. Such actions can eliminate or overlay significant content and thereby corrupt the record.

It is also relatively easy in an on-line environment-and equally confusing for purposes of preserving information integrity-for an author (or user) to make available concurrently multiple representations of what he or she considers to be the same work, providing no definition of a canonical version and viewing all representations as having equal quality and validity. To address these problems, a wide range of cryptographic techniques, such as watermarking, already exist for various kinds of digital information objects.

These could serve well to mark and identify specific, canonical versions and editions of textual, audio and visual works, and to establish trusted, protected channels of distribution for those objects. However, the standards and infrastructure and the policies and practices for applying such techniques to the creation of fixed versions of digital information objects still need considerable development.

Absent such development and the fixity of information that would result, digital archives face considerable challenges in trying to preserve the integrity of digital objects.

Some kinds of digital objects present the problem of fixity of information in yet another way. An increasing number of networked information resources are better modeled, not in terms of versions or editions of works, but as continuously updated databases. The financial communities also depend on large, continuously updated databases. There is no natural way to fix these resources at the database level, no natural set of publication points for the objects as a whole. Their integrity, or singularity, as databases resides in the coherence of the database as a whole and in the continuousness of the updates.

To preserve the integrity of such information resources, the complete record of changes has to be built into the design of the database and fixed at the record level. In the absence of such a preservation-oriented design, digital archives may have no choice but to fix the database artificially in time and capture a series of snapshots of its state at periodic intervals as a way of preserving its integrity. Information objects come into being and acquire their distinctiveness in relation to various other objects in an information space.

For an object to maintain its integrity, its wholeness and singularity, one must be able to locate it definitively and reliably over time among other objects. Systems of citation, description and classification provide the necessary means of reference so that one can consistently discover, identify and retrieve relevant objects. Such systems traditionally include bibliographies, catalogs, indices, data dictionaries, directory systems, finding aids and the like, all of which collect, assemble and organize references to bodies of work. Creators of these resources are already extending them with such innovations, for example, as the use of the 856 field in bibliographic records, to incorporate reference to digital objects.

Moreover, in the electronic environment, there are also emerging sophisticated tools for automatically gathering and presenting in new kinds of products referential information from textual, image, sound, video and other kinds of digital objects. To meet the test of consistent reference, however, citations to digital objects from these various manually and automatically generated sources must over time reliably identify the works to which they refer. One way of establishing confidence in a reference system is to generate citations in the first place- either manually or automatically-from the self-referential information that a work itself carries with it, perhaps in a header, a digital envelope or some other distinct part of the digital object. Unfortunately, except for documents marked up to the standard of the Text Encoding Initiative, few digital objects today contain self-referential information that meets conventional citation quality.

Matching citation and digital work to meet the test of consistent reference thus is difficult. Moreover, reliably identifying multiple versions and editions of works in electronic form remains a persistent reference problem. There are several factors contribute to the unique identification of digital information objects. Two of the most important factors are the Uniform Resource Name (URN) and the Uniform Resource Locator (URL).

The URL refers to the specific place where a digital object resides and is currently the dominant method of object location on the World Wide Web. The weakness of the URL, however, is that it may frequently change, especially as an object migrates from one machine to the next. By contrast, a name, the URN, is supposed to apply uniquely and permanently to a distinct object and to designate it independently of its particular location at any point in time. URNs today exist more in concept than in practice. Thus, resolving the name and location for variant digital works and thereby providing consistent reference to them means moving from a conceptual design of the relation between names and locations to an operational reality through the implementation of naming authorities, which assign URNs, and and the development of digital services that translate names into currently valid URLs. In order to provide a consistent means of reference for digital objects, systems of citation, description and classification will need to dispense more than name and location information.

The IETF framework provides a general category for additional reference information in what it calls Uniform Resource Characteristics (URCs). Among the kinds of information that a reference system might provide under this general category is information about the intellectual property rights governing the use of a particular object and its cost. For archival purposes, however, there are two other qualities of digital information objects that a reference system must take into account. Provenance has become one of the central organizing concepts of modern archival science. The assumption underlying the principle of provenance is that the integrity of an information object is partly embodied in tracing from where it came.

To preserve the integrity of an information object, digital archives must preserve a record of its origin and chain of custody. For some information objects, the formal process of publication creates a trusted channel of distribution and serves to establish a sophisticated record of provenance, at least from the creator through the point of release. In the digital environment, the problems of documenting provenance through a record of publication are bound up with the problems of fixity, and particularly with issues involved in tracing multiple versions and editions, as described above.

Outside the path of publication, however, there are several other channels of information creation and distribution, including tracing the path of migration within their own organization, that digital archives need to document in order to preserve the integrity of digital objects in their custody. First, there is a chain of provenance from individuals, a trail which has comprised a traditional concern of archivists. In the digital environment, as in other domains, individuals produce and accrete much information that relates to their private lives and to their public roles and responsibilities, including their means of livelihood.

Among the kinds of information objects that may count as personal records in digital form are electronic mail, notes, manuscripts, journals, photographs or videos, and databases of personal finances. A second kind of digital information flow that requires special attention with respect to provenance are those mediated or governed by corporate information systems. The archival challenge for establishing the provenance of such objects is to find ways to preserve an understanding of the corporate policies and processes and roles and responsibilities thus represented in the information system and its products. Third, there is the chain of provenance that traces information, particularly scientific data, to a source in electronic instrumentation.

In some cases, the instrumentation produces data in the service of individual experiments or of clinical practice; in other cases, remote sensors gather streams of observational data about physical systems in space or on earth. Of course, one ultimately accounts for the origin of the resulting data in the design and conduct of the experiment or clinical service, or in the character of the remote sensing program. However, the use of the instrumentation creates a special requirement to trace the provenance of the data to the design characteristics of the instrument itself. The data are a direct product of and derive their meaning and usefulness from the calibration, units of measure, sampling rate, conditions of recording and other relevant features embedded in the technology of the instrument.

Finally, a concern for provenance in preserving the integrity of digital information means that digital archives must document what happens to the information within their own organizations. They must keep a record of migration activity, and particularly of the transformations they make to keep information objects current with new technologies for use. The fifth attribute of information integrity that bears on the preservation of digital information objects is their context, the ways in which they interact with elements in the wider digital environment. The context of digital information includes a technical dimension, a dimension of linkage to other objects, a communication dimension, and a wider social dimension.

Digital archives must be attentive to the ways in which each of these contextual dimensions affects the integrity of the objects in their care. First, to specify the technical context of digital information is to specify its hardware and software dependencies. Digital objects, by nature, require the use of computer hardware and software to create and use them. In some cases, an object may be closely dependent on a configuration of technology. For example, a particular digital document may require a particular word processing program running on a machine with a special kind of computer processing chip and operating system.

Other objects, such as an image file, may be readable using a variety of software programs, but may be stored on disk in a format that is readable only with a special computer. For still other objects, like World Wide Web documents marked-up in HTML, the hardware and software dependencies may be specified in very general terms because they are readable with a software browser that is available on almost any hardware platform.

The archival challenges for preserving the integrity of these various kinds of objects are, on the one hand, to represent faithfully the context of the objects in terms of their hardware and software dependencies and, on the other hand, to overcome, through appropriate migration efforts, those dependencies that threaten to hinder future use. At present, there appears to be no good archiving solution; a possible stop-gap measure would be to treat the network in terms of its component parts and to take periodic snapshots of the individual WWW objects.

The communications medium comprises a third dimension of the context of digital information. The character and integrity of digital information objects depends, in part, on their mode of distribution. Material distributed on CD-ROM, for example, has a set of file format and other characteristics that set it apart from material distributed in, say, networked form. As digital materials increasingly come into being and subsist in an electronically networked environment, contextual features of the network, such as bandwidth and security, will account for characteristics of the digital objects. Increasing bandwidth, for example, will stimulate the production and dissemination of high-bandwidth digital materials such as full-motion video.

Similarly, improved security on the network will encourage the conduct of a wide variety of confidential transactions. As network-based objects, such as video and records of confidential transactions, make their way into digital repositories, an archival account of their integrity must include an account of the features of the network context that supports their existence. The wider social environment plays a significant contextual role that contributes to the integrity of digital information objects.

Networked information, for example, depends on specific policy and implementation decisions that address the bandwidth, security and other qualities of the network and related technical infrastructure. Electronic mail is subject to a variety of social distinctions when, in some contexts, it is used to convey highly personal messages among friends and, in other contexts, is a vehicle for formal communication among academic or business colleagues.

One might account for digital business records, too, in the social context of the political and organizational regime in which they were generated. Indeed, the social context of digital information objects is an expression of what one might characterize in other terms as the interests of stakeholders in those objects. Digital information objects acquire the qualities of content, fixity, reference, provenance and context-and thereby their integrity-as they move through a life cycle in a series of relationships with parties, or stakeholders, who have specific interests in their creation, management, dissemination, use or retention.

The initial stakeholder in a digital information object is, of course, the creator of its content. Following creation, a digital information object may pass through a series of gateways of increasingly public release and access. Some digital information objects (like videos of family picnics or private journals) may never be released beyond the initial creator; others will be limited to an immediate circle, which may or may not be physically co-located with the creator. Still other objects will be very widely disseminated. Once a creator fixes a digital information object by releasing it, for either personal or wider use, the object invites various other kinds of stakeholder interests.

Depending on the extent of the release and the nature of the object, users and other stakeholders may refer to it, index it or cite it. Still others may acquire, license or otherwise take custody of it to edit and publish it, to invoke it as evidence of a transaction or perhaps, as in the case of scientific data, to study, analyze and report it. They will all use it in the context of specific hardware and software applications and perhaps link it to related objects. And eventually during the course of its life, a digital information object may attract the interest of stakeholders, such as a digital libraries, which serve as collectors/disseminators of information objects.

What unites all these various stakeholders, of course, is their particular interest in adding to or making use of the value of digital information objects. However, the integrity of information objects in the digital environment is today so fragile that as stakeholders disseminate, use, reuse, recreate and re-disseminate various kinds of digital information, they can easily, even inadvertently, destroy valuable information, corrupt the cultural record, and ultimately thwart the pursuit of knowledge that is their common end. Against such a danger, a safety-net is needed to ensure that digital information objects with long-term cultural and intellectual value survive the expressions of stakeholder interest with their integrity intact. Among the stakeholders serving as collector/disseminators, those who perform archival functions provide just such a safety-net.

Digital archives build and maintain reliable collections of well-defined digital information objects and they preserve the features-content, fixity, reference, provenance and context-that give those objects their integrity and enduring value. Such an archival network will establish a critical part of the foundation needed to support a burgeoning, but still fragile, national and international knowledge economy. As the networked environment for digital information expands and matures, intense interactions among the parties with stakes in digital information are providing the opportunity and stimulus for new stakeholders to emerge and add value, and for the relationships and division of labor among existing stakeholders to assume new forms.

For example, naming authorities for digital information objects are being organized, creators are assuming the role of publishers, publishers are contemplating the construction of digital archives, and collector/disseminators are facing the need to resolve the names and locations of digital objects. Moreover, all of the stakeholders, including the new ones who are emerging, are exercising their various functions simultaneously in relation to particular digital information objects. That is, for example, the creator of an object may retain a financial or other stake in its dissemination and use for an extended period, just as a publisher/disseminator of the object exercises the same or similar interest.

Similarly, stakeholders acting as collectors/disseminators may retain an interest in the continuing use of the object, at the same time as they or other stakeholders acting as digital archives take steps to preserve it for future use. In a time of such sustained flux and change, during which these various divisions of labor are taking shape, the most effective and affordable strategy for developing a system of digital archives is to assume a distributed, rather than centralized, structure for collecting digital information objects, protecting their integrity over the long term, and retaining them for future use. A distributed structure, built on a foundation of electronic networks, places archival responsibility with those who presumably care most about and have the greatest understanding of the value of particular digital information objects.

Moreover, such a structure locates the economic and cultural incentives where they are most likely to prompt those preserving digital information to respond with the greatest agility to the changing digital landscape and to the shifting tides of technology. Effective structures for digital archives in a distributed network will surely take various forms and will include corporations, federations and consortia, each of which may specialize in the archiving of digital information and range over regional and national boundaries.

Both informal collaborations (associations and alliances) and formal partnerships among contractors and subcontractors, will also surely arise, in which responsibilities for archiving are allocated among various other interests in digital information. Moreover, shared interests in, for example, intellectual discipline, in type of information, in function, such as storage or cataloging, and even interests in the output of information within national boundaries will all form a varied and rich basis for the kinds of formal and informal interactions that lead to the design of particular archival organizations.

In the end, existing archival organizations may successfully adapt their current roles and responsibilities to changing needs, existing archival roles and responsibilities may be redistributed among other kinds of organizations with stakes in digital information, and focused attention on the division of labor in the digital information economy will lead to the emergence and growth of new kinds of archival structures.

Creators of knowledge in other spheres depend on past knowledge and regularly acknowledge their responsibility to add to the enduring record when they publish their own ideas and findings. As the properties and usefulness of other kinds of information objects become more widely known, the ability in the digital environment to reuse and repackage these objects may generate revenue or other benefits. Creators, owners or providers of these objects, including some publishers, who may not have otherwise counted long-term preservation among their key responsibilities, may thus be more inclined to do so and may either assume the responsibility themselves or find a qualified partner to do so.

Among potential partners, they will likely find libraries, archives or similar agencies, which have specific collection agendas and will seek to take or share responsibility for preserving organized collections of digital materials. The second organizing principle calls, in effect, for a fail-safe mechanism. A variety of factors-budgetary constraints, reorganization of priorities or focus, change of business, the need to go out of existence, or expiration of copyright- might prompt custodians to neglect, abandon or destroy their collections of digital information. No distributed system of digital archives will afford effective protection of electronic information unless it provides for a powerful rescue function allowing one agency, acting in the long-term public interest of protecting the cultural record, to override another's neglect of or active interest in abandoning or destroying parts of that record.

Digital archives operating normally and those operating in fail-safe mode differ mainly in the rights and obligations they have with respect to rescuing materials that have fallen in jeopardy because a custodian no longer accepts prescrvation responsibility. Section 108 of the 1976 Copyright Act of the United States defines the rights and obligations for libraries and archives operating normally to preserve copies of printed materials. The proposed revision of the copyright law reserves to libraries and archives similar rights and duties for digital materials.

However, neither in its present form nor in its proposed revision does the Copyright Act provide a legal foundation defining the rights and duties that must come into play to facilitate and encourage an aggressive rescue function. The Copyright Act, in fact, may not provide the best legal and institutional framework for establishing fail-safe mechanisms for digital archives. However, such a framework is urgently needed because we know that one of the greatest dangers to the long life of digital information is the ease with which it can be abandoned and then deliberately or inadvertently destroyed.

One appropriate foundation for an archival fail-safe mechanism against this danger might rest in articulating for the various domains of intellectual property-on analogy from the domain of real estate-a definition of the concept of abandonment and of the rights and duties that follow for digital archives operating in fail-safe mode when they can show that present custodians have abandoned, or are in the process of abandoning, culturally valuable objects. Other means of providing a fail-safe mechanism for digital archives also exist, however. Users of archived information in electronic form and of archival services relating to that information need to have assurance that a digital archives is what it says that it is and that the information stored there is safe for the long term.

Appropriate organizations and individuals need to begin now developing such standards and criteria, including standard methods for a repository to declare its existence as a digital archives and therefore its intentions to preserve the contents over which it has custody, and for describing what the archives contains and what services it provides. The certification process must also address the standards and best practices for other dimensions of archival operation, including selection and accessioning of material, its storage and access and the engineering of the systems environment.

Archives cannot save all information objects; they must appraise and select for retention the most valuable items. Selection processes for archives of all kinds—paper and digital-are matters of intellectual judgment about what to include and save and what to exclude. Criteria for such judgments are largely tied to the intrinsic qualities of the material and many of the criteria that have proven useful in the paper world will no doubt translate to and prove equally effective in the digital environment. In general, selection criteria include an appraisal of the content of the object-its subject and discipline-in relation to the collection goals of the digital archives, the quality and uniqueness of the object, its accessibility in terms of available hardware and software, its present value and its likely future value.

Search and retrieval in large universes of diverse digital materials is the subject of very active computer science research, but search and retrieval today against a rapidly expanding universe of materials in all forms-digital, paper, microform—remains difficult, and the relatively primitive systems currently in operation may, in the short term at least, inhibit the effective selection of materials for digital archives. Redundancy of information is also important for effective selection. Selectors need to know before accepting an object where a copy of record is stored and if and where additional copies are distributed either as backup or for more efficient retrieval.

Such understandings remain in relatively short supply in some measure because the educational processes for wedding selection and technical skills still need to be devised and perfected. In larger measure, however, technical understandings are deficient because the digital environment is so immature that the dependencies of information objects on underlying hardware and software are still in many respects unknown. Finally, selection for digital archives must be a continuing process. Given the need to migrate digital information regularly from its hardware and software environment, the stimulus and occasion will recur to reappraise the value of the material being migrated.

Materials may lose value over time and may need to be withdrawn and discarded. Hard decisions may also be necessary about how and whether digital objects migrate if changes in a technical environment force alters what is preserved so that it differs in fundamental ways from what existed in the original object. Digital archives thus need to formulate and implement policies and practices for ongoing appraisal. Once an information object is identified for inclusion in a digital archives, it needs to be accessioned, that is, prepared for the archives. The accession process involves both describing and cataloging selected objects, including their provenance and context, and securing them for storage and access.

Standards for description are well developed for certain kinds of materials that are likely to appear in digital archives, such as monographs and serials. Because of the high degree of standardization, one might reasonably expect such descriptions eventually to accompany the digital object, thus simplifying the accessioning process. For other kinds of materials, such as WWW pages, motion video and multimedia, relevant attributes are less well understood. Standards of description are less well practiced and one cannot reasonably expect satisfactory descriptive material to accompany the digital object. In all cases, special attention is needed in the accession process to creating, describing and tracking the versions of the object in the digital archives to satisfy the various requirements for display and other forms of access and for long-term storage.

If material is to be deaccessioned then public declarations need to be made to that effect, particularly if it is the last known copy, so that rescue efforts by others can proceed if appropriate. In the accession process, selected digital objects also need to be made secure for indefinite future use. A digital archives may need to establish access controls for its information objects and the means for authenticating them to future users. Establishing access controls involves setting terms and conditions for authorized use by specific users or classes of users.

For certain extreme cases, such as rescued objects still under intellectual property protection, there may be no authorized uses for certain periods of time except for internal use within the digital archives to ensure that the object will be accessible in the future. Authentication, which may make use of cryptography, provides verification that a digital object is what it purports to be and contains the contents that the author/creator or publisher originally intended.

One of the characteristics of materials in digital archives may need to be that they contain a digital digest or signature that users can independently verify to assure themselves that the object is unchanged from its archival state. The storage operation in digital archives attends primarily to the media level formatting of information objects. Primary considerations include levels of hierarchy and redundancy. In any digital archives, there may be multiple levels of storage graded to levels of expected use and needed performance in retrieval. Little used material may be stored most efficiently off-line, usually in tape format.

For objects in high demand, where retrieval time is at a premium, on-line storage in magnetic media may serve best.

In a distributed network, they may need to be stored on-line in multiple locations. An intermediate solution is near-line storage, where information objects may be stored on optical or tape media and loaded in a jukebox. Retrieval time in near-line storage systems suffers by comparison to on-line storage, but is considerably more responsive to user demand than off-line storage. Digital archives may use any or all of these methods. The most sophisticated systems combine the resources so that objects in use or recent use are stored on-line and, as they age from the time of most recent use, they move to near-line storage and then eventually off-line.

Another important storage consideration is redundancy. In a system that is completely dependent on the interaction of various kinds and levels of hardware and software, failure in any one of the subsystems could mean the loss or corruption of the information object. Effective storage management thus means providing for redundant copies of the archived objects as an insurance against loss. Depending on the copyright status of the objects, digital archives may choose to make backup copies on their own or to make arrangements for other sites, which hold the same object, in the network of digital archives to serve as backup, or they may choose to do both.

Providing access to digital information in a distributed network environment means above all that digital archives are connected to networks using appropriate protocols and with bandwidth suitable for delivering the information their control. Digital archives have an obligation to maintain the information in a form so that users over the network can find it with appropriate retrieval engines and view, print, listen to or otherwise use it with appropriate output devices.

Changing Professionals

There are a number of reasons why the library and information science profession is undergoing change, and it is urgent that there is a suitable response from practitioners, the professional associations and those who educate for the profession. The rationality of the library in many ways represents the description of nature idealized by the institution of positivist science.' The librarian-god becomes the guardian of rationality and knowledge. The tendency to set the user aside can be explained within this paradigm, as the librarian seeks to exercise rationality and control over the collection and the user can be seen as a chaotic interrupter.

Today's 'user-centredness' often is reduced to the nature of the user's relationship with the information system, rather than the user's engagement with the universe of knowledge creation and information behaviour. An educator in LIS is engaged in preparing people for a career in the field. This requires a concern with the wider social context within which these careers will unfold over time. The unpredictability of the present environment makes both these tasks very difficult. Many factors in the sophisticated and complex society in which we now find ourselves have compelled a substantial reassessment of the educational requirements for careers in information management.

These include changing human information behaviours, education and work competencies, and the increase in the value of information as a strategic and economic commodity. A strong tradition in LIS is that of service - for the purpose of education, enculturation, social uplift - as well as the notion of the development of social capital. There is no doubt that information workers carry a professional responsibility that is of utmost importance in today's society, although the scope of this responsibility is now much broader than previously. With the twin effects of global cultural imperialism conveyed through the media, and endemic information overload that is simply too much for most to deal with, information workers can play a role in reducing cultural and ideological differences because of their influence over information. There is no doubt that the situation that LIS now faces is complex, and many issues remain unexplained and therefore cannot be dealt with by the present dominant paradigm.

Most LIS educational programs both here and internationally have dealt with such anomalies in a piecemeal way, adding various courses such as web page design, records management, database construction and the like in order to increase the job opportunities for graduates. Incremental change seems to be what people can handle most comfortably. Any large change is psychologically threatening, and in any case, the necessary information to predict the consequences of action simply isn't available. This phrase describes very well the developments in LIS education. The use of different titles and terms in education for LIS professionals is an example of 'disjointed incrementalism'.

In LIS, when this has happened, we have mostly attempted to react only after the event, which is a frequent way of dealing with catastrophe. Collaboration, convergence and diversification are suggested by Wilson as means of survival.

Librarians are on a social mission to protect rights of access to information. The cultural and social location of the origin of information needs to be taken into account: information is a product of its society. This is, of course, related to the issue of social responsibility mentioned above. Information professionals can no longer be neutral. Access to ICTs (which support globalisation) is not global or democratic. Theoretically ICTs can build a worldwide network that breaks down the boundaries between countries and removes the cultural barriers between people from different cultures.

In reality, this is not the case: not while there are six billion people on the planet, and only about one billion have regular access to the internet, and the rest are not likely to in their lifetimes. Globalisation ensures that masses of information are available internationally, but it also has the side issue of privatisation of information access - increasingly this costs more.

Information is an enabler, but globalisation is making it a purchasable good. This is what creates a digital divide. They are further of the opinion that growing privatisation of information may cause libraries to be bypassed altogether - and this view was expressed in 1988, before the widespread use of the internet which has in fact emphasised this. A critical environmental change is the increase in the value of information as a strategic commodity. Information's role in creating power and wealth is attracting the attention of powerful new players - and new competition for LIS.

The commodification of information and knowledge not only has an impact on LIS, but profound implications for social values and the community at large - outcomes which information professionals, including librarians, need to be considering now. Many LIS problems are interdisciplinary - but we show a reluctance to address such issues. Multi-disciplinarity leads to more interdisciplinary work. Most programs are too narrow to address the increasing challenges of the profession, concentrating instead on the identification of core.

There is some growth: the infusion of multi-disciplinary perspectives results as LIS educators conduct research with people from cognate fields, and when they offer joint programs/courses with other academic departments. Such developments could encourage a fresh examination of LIS, and an appreciation of the field as a kind of meta-discipline, dealing as it does with knowledge. Attracting the 'right' type of student to LIS courses is a dilemma in and of itself; ensuring that they gain employment on graduation is critical. Willard and Mychalyn looked at the relationship between available jobs, qualifications of LIS graduates and the successful applicants.

A knowledge base is most likely to offer the most to a neophyte information worker than a collection of rapidly dated skills, as the graduate must be able to respond to new and uncharted problems during his/her career. One aspect is that such a paradigm will be inclusive. Even more significantly, such a paradigm should be reflective of a different world view towards the processes of information management, and, as such, identify the core knowledge of the field.

As a result, as social and economic circumstances change, there is no unified body of theory to provide a lens with which to view new problems and deal with them. The traditional focus of LIS has not been on information at all but rather on its containers - books, journals, maps, and so on. It acquires, describes, stores and disseminates them without much concern for how their intellectual content is used. It is the information itself with which information professionals should be concerned. Just what this information is, and how it can be managed, is clarified further below, as this is a pivotal point.

In passing, it is worth noting that the future of libraries themselves (as storehouses of physical objects) is incidental or even irrelevant to the profession. In librarianship, there is a paradox in that we seek to describe the content of documents in words that best express the content, without studying linguistics or semiotics, or understanding the social construction of knowledge, or the contextual base for meaning. Social issues, such as access, information's contribution to social uplift, the role of information policies in organisations and countries, and the relationship between society and technology is vital for a professional and international perspective.

The educational ramifications of these changes are considerable. There needs to be more orientation toward the corporate and information industry constituency; more emphasis on data and information structuring and the design of information systems; development of a more entrepreneurial and market orientation; development of a more international orientation; and the development of a core competency that is general to information professions and not specific to librarianship, in recognition of the great employment mobility of information professionals. Undergraduate education in LIS is a fairly recent phenomenon, and has not been successful in most parts of the world where it has been tried.

At most, LIS undergraduate courses have been offered as electives to other degrees, notably education. In general, such individual courses have not been seen as offering essential skills in the information society. There are some immediate problems with such a proposal which cannot be fully explored here, such as the tradition-bound university and the conflict between striving for graduate-level scholarship, encouraging students to pursue research which advances the profession, and satisfying employers who pay most attention to skills-level details and competencies. There are different career stages which require different educational outcomes, as well.

For the foreseeable future, most e-publishing will involve scientific, technical, professional, and academic information, as well as some original fiction. Librarians and others involved in digital asset management will have to preserve at least some of this material for future reference, since it is expected that original works will be created and many of these may exist only in electronic form. E-books are not a historical artifact or anomaly, but a new form of content conveyance. Growth, while steady, may be slow because of competing technical standards, digital rights management, definitional issues, and restructuring within traditional publishing, as creators, existing publishing houses, and software companies position and reposition themselves in a changing market.

Since the advent of disc- and tape-based digital storage in the 1960s, we have seen the evolution and proliferation of more than 200 different data storage formats-from large- and small-diameter fixed discs, to flexible diskettes of every size, to compact and video discs. During this time, media have decreased in size and increased in storage capacity, from 1 kilobyte of data to 40 gigabytes of data, with the first terabyte discs imminent. No single format has existed for more than a decade, which has necessitated the recording and rerecording of information on new media to allow access by current computing systems.

This trend has also affected the entertainment industry as it evolved from records, to tapes in cassettes and cartridges, to compact discs (CDs) and now to digital video discs (DVDs). At the Rochester Institute of Technology, files stored on 8-inch flexible diskettes from word processors of the 1970s are unreadable-not because of their condition but because readers for that medium are unavailable. Libraries and information repositories face a continuing challenge in maintaining files on currently supported storage hardware and media and in currently supported file formats for currently supported operating systems that require structured data organization. An electronic book, or e-book, is the presentation of electronic files on digital displays.

Although the term "e-book" implies book-oriented information, other content can also be displayed on such devices. Static text and images are typically displayed, but moving imagery and audio are also presented. E-book files can be provided as recorded units (discs) or downloaded from digital repositories (including Web sites) to desktop computer monitors, laptop screens, portable digital assistants (PDAs or Palm-type devices), cell phones with expanded displays, pocket pagers, or dedicated digital reading devices (also currently called "e-books"). The e-book production cycle begins when an author creates an original work and submits it to a publisher.

An e-book distributor manages the protected file. The e-book publisher or distributor transfers the work to an e-book retailer, who sells the protected e-book online and offers buyers a "key" to decrypt and read the work. A buyer connects with a retailer's Web site and purchases the work, after unlocking the file with the digital rights key and downloading it to read on an e-book reading device. The word "e-book" is actually a misnomer. The device can display magazine content (e-magazine) and newspaper content (e-newspaper), as well as electronic directories, catalogues, and other material. The display device is independent of the content. However, a distinguishing characteristic of books, magazines, and newspapers is the size of the page-all must adjust to the device's screen size, which is currently about the same as that of the page of a standard hardcover book. A Web site is a collection of HTML-coded files and other files (image, audio, video) in computer code that are displayed on a screen using a browser application program.

The browser (e.g., Netscape Navigator or Internet Explorer) translates the coded data into displayable typographic and image elements and presents them to the viewer. An important aspect of such sites is the ability to click on defined elements that then automatically display other Web sites ("hyperlinks"). A computer linked to the Internet functions like an e-book does and thus inherits many of the challenges associated with long-term use and preservation of Web sites. Consider the problem of how to identify and find a Web site.

Web sites have addresses so that viewers can connect from one to another. Such addresses have been used as bibliographic references or identifiers. After only a few years, those address may no longer be active. This presents another challenge to the preservation of information, because it is not expected that most e-books will be delivered via media (discs, for example) but rather through connections to the Internet or proprietary sources-wired or wireless. Thus, the content may be unfindable or unavailable for downloading.

While it may be expected that libraries and other information repositories might be backups for Web-based content acquisition, libraries and information repositories will have to store such information on some form of storage media, and, unless standards evolve, they may require a plethora of different reading devices. An alternative scenario would have libraries serve as portals to any number of commercial sites. However, the likelihood of long-term preservation by commercial enterprises may not be as assured as is preservation by certain libraries.

Thus, libraries and other data repositories hold the responsibility of long-term preservation. Computer operating systems are usually aligned to structured storage systems that record coded data. The storage of digital data will require a dynamic form of preservation, and a new definition of "archival" may have to be developed. The concept of long-term storage of a paper- or photographic-based item that remains unchanged over time may not be applicable with electronic publishing. Instead, the information will have to be re-recorded on new media to be used with existing file formats and computer operating systems as storage media degrade and systems, formats, and encoding systems evolve.

There are programs that convert from one encoding system to another. Over time, these programs will become more reliable and allow data to be reformatted to the current standard approach. But the conversion will have to take place in order to keep the information in a "current" format. Usually there is a two-year transition between one form of storage and its successor. The size of the page-or the screen-is the defining property of e-books. This was fundamentally enabled by the "portable-monitor".

Most e-books are capable of downloading and storing text and displaying it in a prescribed format that is intended to mimic that of a typical printed book. The text is usually displayed one screenful at a time and in most models is advanced or regressed a screenful at a time with arrow buttons. Some models do not have page numbers; in this case, a screenful of text may be considered a page. Page orientation can be adjusted with some brands.

Most electronic books also have "advance" features that allow users to move quickly forward or backward as if paging through a printed book. The books are battery powered but also come with electrical adapters. Rechargeable batteries can last from 10 to 40 hours, depending on the brand and whether backlighting is used. The size and resolution capabilities of e-books vary. They can support text as well as black-and-white images such as graphs, line art, and newspaper-resolution photos. Gray-scale images are not supported with most brands.

All the current e-books are black and white; there are few colour models. Within two years, most models will display gray-scale images and colour and also play sound and video. Most e-books come with proprietary software that is used to transfer data to and from the e-book as well as to allow downloading from Internet-based or proprietary services. The most significant advance toward a paperless world will be portable displays-lightweight, rugged, operating for hours using lightweight batteries, with high resolution and contrast. In the late 1980s, LCDs were incorporated in the first laptop computers, and today the typical laptop computer includes a 12- to 14-inch, full-color LCD with good resolution.

LCD-based flat-panel displays are smaller and lighter, use less power, and discharge fewer electromagnetic emissions than do their cathode ray tube (CRT) counterparts. There are a number of issues and organizations involved in developing standards. These involve markup languages, identification, and metadata as well as hardware and software standards. The hypertext markup language (HTML) and portable document format (PDF) standards continue as dominant document formats on the Internet, but are not necessarily perfect standards for information delivered on hand-held devices such as e-books.

HTML displays can have difficulty with consistency and Acrobat displays the equivalent of printed pages, which may be oversized for most small devices. Both of these limitations are being addressed: HTML is metamorphosing into extensible markup language (XML) to allow more consistent reformatting on different screens, and Adobe is integrating PDF and such reformatting into future versions of PDF. A PDF file is truly a portable document. It can be generated from just about any application and keeps all typographic formatting, graphics, layout, and page integrity intact.

Because the PDF embeds fonts, the recipient need not have the fonts that were used by the document creator. Graphics are compressed, which allows PDF files to be very small for transmission over networks. The reader software runs on most computers and is free-downloaded from Adobe's Web site. In 1998, the National Institute for Standards and Technology (NIST) of the U.S. Department of Commerce formed the Open E-Book Standards Committee (OEBSC) to promote a standard e-book format. The Open E-Book Publication Structure, developed by OEBSC, defines the format for content converted from print to electronic form. The Electronic Book Exchange (EBX) Working Group is establishing copyright protection and distribution standards.

The Open eBook Forum (OeBF) is an international, nonprofit trade organization whose mission is to promote the development of the e-publishing market. The Open eBook Authoring Group, made up of the major e-book reader manufacturers, a few large publishers, and Microsoft, among others, released the first Open eBook Specification in September 1999-a specification based on XML.

The Open Ebook Standards Project, led by the Association of American Publishers (AAP), several leading publishers, and Andersen Consulting (now Accenture), released the results of an intensive effort to establish recommendations and voluntary standards. Experts have been working with AAP to develop standards for numbering and metadata, and to identify publisher requirements for digital rights management, three areas critical to the growth of the market. The new standards specify a numbering system based on the Digital Object Identifier, an internationally supported system suited for identifying digital content and discovering it through network services.

The numbering recommendations allow for identification of e-books in multiple formats and facilitate the sale of parts of e-books, and they also work with existing systems such as the ISBN to allow publishers to migrate to the new system. The metadata standard has extended ONIX, the existing international publishing standard for content metadata, to include the information needed to support the new numbering system and e-book-specific data. With ONIX, publishers will be able to provide their metadata to (r)e-tailers, conversion houses, and digital rights partners. Indexing of the metadata will make e-books easier to find in online catalogues.

AAP also released a comprehensive description of digital rights management (DRM) features needed to enable the variety of new products and business models publishers want to offer. There are numerous proprietary software solutions being offered to translate digital e-book files for the many competing reader platforms. Most solutions incorporate security features to protect copyright owners (that is, the file cannot be printed or copied). It may be that reading devices may display some of all of these formats, but one or two probably will become clear standards. Publishers have already restricted their market through the use of a reading device.

Unless a very inexpensive reader is developed and becomes universally available, this market cannot evolve. The information for these readers must also be standardized and pervasive. It is not that we do not have standards-we may have too many of them. Publishers are implementing a range of strategies, partnerships, and experiments with delivery and packaging. In 1995, book publishers produced thousands of multimedia computer CDs with interactive features, pictures, and sounds, but consumers did not accept the new electronic works.

Personal computers were not as pervasive; technical standards caused innumerable problems running the programs; and few personal computers had CD-ROM drives. Multimedia has grown into a significant market as standards evolved and the base of computer users expanded. Major book publishers, technology companies, online booksellers, and new e-book middlemen are investing in the future market of digital books. Authors may see electronic books as a way to free themselves from dependence on publishers and to sell books directly to consumers. Publishers may see an opportunity to eliminate printers and bookstores.

Online booksellers are moving into the publishers' business, printing digitized books themselves and selling their own electronic editions. Startup companies sell the contents of books through digital archives of thousands of books and periodicals available on-line, liberated from the constraints of time and shelf space. Publishers now see e-books as incremental sales to computer-savvy adults and the next generation of readers. A publisher's ultimate responsibility is to get the work to the largest-possible audience and the Internet has that potential. But no one knows what an electronic book is worth. Some publishers are setting prices for e-books just below those of their printed equivalents, but others charge much less.

Digital publishing presents an opportunity for authors and publishers to develop a much closer connection to consumers than they have in the past. There will still be retailers, but certainly the middleman component may be smaller. Some publishers are already selling digital books directly to consumers as customized editions with modular contents, especially in the educational market. Each of the main e-book contenders is pursuing a different strategy and competing for publishers' digital books. NetLibrary sells electronic books to libraries via online access to the digital version of the book on their computer servers. Users can search the contents of books in the online collection, but they cannot copy or print the books.

Public and university libraries and some corporations are now customers. The future of digital publishing will also be shaped by the competition among three technology companies hoping to set the standards for publishing and reading books on screens. Microsoft, Adobe Systems, and Gemstar-TV Guide International are working to convince publishers and readers that their format is the most secure from copying, convenient to use, and easy on the eyes. Microsoft and Adobe Systems produce competing software programs intended to make reading on a screen easier on the eyes, and both have announced alliances intended to strengthen their respective positions.

Xerox, IBM, and others now sell machines that in minutes can churn out single, bound copies of paperback or even hardcover books. The output is virtually indistinguishable from that of traditional printing presses. In traditional printing, hundreds of copies must be produced to make a print-run cost-effective. This constraint does not hold for on-demand printing; as a result, some low-selling books that would have passed out of print are staying in print longer, and a few books that might not have found publishers now have done so.

Although the publisher does not receive revenue from these subsequent uses or sales, the reader may develop an affinity for the author or subject, and this may stimulate future sales. Magazines are routinely passed around. Readers of e-publications who wish to save issues for future reference may not be able to do so and may find that the e-book readers do not have external storage. Periodical publishers have an interesting problem with regard to digital rights management, and that is they want to protect their content, but advertising rates in periodicals is in large part based on "pass along" copies.

Publishers are fearful of e-book piracy and of the thought that books could be swapped like MP3 files over the Internet. Adobe must demonstrate a secure option or it will lose the support of major publishers. But Elcomsoft also showed that it could break Microsoft protection systems. Many feel it is better to show the vulnerability of such systems in an open forum than to drive it underground. The result of the ensuing argument and debate was a ruling that essentially defined e-books as a new medium of communication, like audio books. There is an interesting privacy issue in that book buyers (at least those who pay in cash) are generally anonymous.

In many cases, e-books will be sold only to a specific device assigned to a specific individual. Civil libertarians may see the irony in the complete democratization of publishing at the expense of privacy. Libraries and other data repositories must take a more active role in shaping the future of e-publishing. Efforts are focused on standards, devices, delivery, security, and commerce; however, almost no consideration is being given to preservation.

The role of university libraries is even more important. It is impossible to imagine a good university without an extensive library. Libraries are assumed to contain materials that present a true picture of the world. Readers have confidence in books they find in libraries. They assume that authors are honest in their presentation of the matter they write about and do not want to trick them. Readers also trust librarians who, they believe, would not collect books written by malicious writers who purposefully distort the image of reality. Knowledge, is therefore, a collection of justified beliefs that correspond with reality.

It seems that librarians rigorously apply themselves to give the public access to a true representation of the world. They insist on the division of the collection into two clearly separated domains, fiction and non-fiction. Fiction denotes imaginary writing, in other words, made-up stories. Nonfiction is restricted to books containing truthful representation of facts. When readers enter the nonfiction section they assume that they have access to knowledge and not mere opinions. Creative works describe imaginary characters and situations, existing only in authors' and readers' minds.

In contrast, knowledge and information is a representation of the world as it really is, perceived by our senses and organised by our minds in a coherent mental picture of the world. Novels describe events that did not really happen. Even in historical novels, which are partly based on facts, the fictional and subjective character of the story is self-evident. In fact, modern librarianship is under pressure to reinvent itself. One of the most radical re-evaluations of the epistemological foundation of librarianship is proposed by Gary P Radford in his article '*Flaubert, Foucault, and the Bibliotheque Fantastique: towards a postmodern epistemology for library science*'. Radford is dissatisfied with the model of the library as a mirror of reality. In his view, the library has existed as an institution that imposed constraints on readers and limited their freedom to explore the world and to express freely their opinions.

In the past, readers visited libraries with the sole purpose of searching for information. Their actions had to take place within rules devised by librarians. Readers had to meet the expectations of librarians and were forced to play the role of those who always wanted to know more. The whole process was highly institutionalised. Only certain forms of knowledge were sanctioned by librarians. Knowledge was systematically organised and there was no room for dissent. Only one side had the right to decide what was 'true': knowledge was intimidating because it was Truth itself, imposing and non-negotiable.

Postmodernism is also a Romantic movement. It is often said that postmodernists reject the great project of the Enlightenment when people wanted to build a civilization based entirely on Reason. If we accept, as postmodernist librarians want to, that every reader is entitled to have his own opinions and is free to read books in any way he finds fit, libraries will lose their reason for existence. In a traditional library, readers are under pressure to accept a rigorous method of searching for information. Books make demands on them. Rules of searching for truth are clearly defined and knowledge is differentiated from opinion. In the past, knowledge was built from coherent and testable statements that corresponded with reality. Hence, broadly speaking, there were three theories of truth depending on what characteristic was stressed.

There is no place in the library for books read for mere entertainment. Reading is identical with thinking, therefore only books that make people think are worth reading. Platonists claim that values and ideas are outside of history and eternally true. Good books are immortal as they reflect eternal Truth. For post-modernists, grand questions about the nature of reality and our place in the universe are pointless. There is no Truth; there are only provisional statements that are neither valid nor invalid. Distinctions between good and evil, beautiful and ugly and true and false are not discernible any more. There are no good books and no bad books. Post-modernist librarians do not pay much attention to collection development.

Books are to be read here and now because they will soon be superseded by new books. Books resemble newspapers in their ephemerality and unimportance. Reading is not a serious engagement and does not lead to the discovery of truth. It is rather like a distraction. A quarrel between Platonists and Postmodernists can be understood as a dispute between conservative and supposedly progressive forces within the fraternity of librarians. Platonists look back into the history of librarianship and they like what they see.

Postmodernists are dissatisfied with the past. Platonists long for the lost Golden Age in librarianship which they locate in the nineteenth century. Then, libraries belonged to the sphere of the sacred. There was a clear pattern in the way public space was organised. A church, cemetery, town hall, school, university, courts and a library were not ordinary places. Their special character was indicated and reinforced by their architectonic style.

Libraries were housed in grandiose buildings that resembled Greek or Roman temples. It was a conscious link to the values that ancient architecture symbolised such as Order, Divine Benevolence, Virtue and Temperance. The Universe was like a book that could be read. Learning was to read the Liber Mundi, or discover a divine pattern and order in the universe. One could see in reading a form of worship, perhaps a divinely inspired activity. It is not an accident, then, that library buildings resembled churches.

Big nineteenth century libraries inspired awe through their imposing structure. In contrast, modern libraries are entirely practical. While libraries in the past had vertical orientation modern libraries are horizontal. They are not meant to be places of special character. Churches, universities, town halls, cemeteries met the same fate. Public space lost meaning and moral significance. Yet, the sacred has not disappeared entirely from our lives. It returned as its own caricature.

The message the new library seems to be sending is that reading is of no consequence and that there is nothing noble in reading. Modern libraries point towards the everyday, mediocrity, secularity, nonsense. Nothing is serious any more, everything is a game, including reading. Most people read for the fun of it. Reading is not a special activity, as in the past, when it was a solitary contemplation of words that represented reality. Postmodernists want to get rid of this allegedly antiquated worldview. They insist that there are no ideals behind appearances; there is only Becoming and not Being; profanum and not sacrum and everything is ordinary.

People are motivated by base instincts, human behaviour is just a power game and nothing is serious any more. Postmodernists dethroned the concepts of Truth, Beauty and Goodness. They do not see the need for any coherent vision of us and our place in the universe. They declare that Truth is dead. They are attached to cultures and distrust civilisation. As Truth is necessarily supra-cultural it can only flourish in an atmosphere in which civilisation is valued more than cultures. What is true must be true in all cultures. Postmodernists distrust Reason. For Platonists, belief in Reason is the core itself of philosophy. Socrates linked

Reason with the Good. God was for him good and rational; He created an orderly world and gave us mental powers to discover this order.

The orderly character of the world may be hidden behind layers of appearances and might be difficult to discover but it is nevertheless there. Western civilisation is based on faith in God's reasonableness and goodness. All these metaphysical assumptions penetrated the lives of our ancestors for centuries. They were necessarily reflected in public institutions, including libraries. Until recently, the pillars of librarianship were firmly grounded in Platonism.

Cultures are supposedly warm and human-friendly while civilisation is cold, brutal and destructive. Cultures are a testament to the diversity of human experience while civilisation is apparently a simplistic invention of the Enlightenment when Reason was glorified, if not deified as during the French Revolution. Feelings are considered superior to Reason which, embodied in science, is being blamed for destroying Nature. Liberals and socialists in the nineteenth century thought that people were essentially good. They hoped that once people broke the social chains imposed on them by cruel political and social systems and freed themselves from material privations they would be able to elevate themselves to a higher level of humanity. Marxists believed in the proletariat, liberals put their trust in ordinary people.

According to post-modernists, there are no Platonic essences any more. No more fixed values independent of man's changing judgment. The people are the ultimate judge of values. No-one has the right, the argument goes, to dictate to the people what they should read, listen to or watch.

People know very well what is good for them. The motives of elitists who insist on canons, standards and values are highly suspicious. What they really want is to restore an ancien régime and create an intellectual apartheid. However, it requires strength of character, discipline and hard work. It is unrealistic to believe that the majority of people are prepared to reject the temptation of mental comfort and to look for Truth at any cost.

Platonism was as a shield against crude pragmatism, vulgar utilitarianism, skepticism, relativism and irrationalism. If libraries are to survive as public institutions working for the common good they must be defended from the postmodernist attack. Once we lose the ability to discern between knowledge and opinion, there will be no need to consult the approved version of the world as presented in library collections. Postmodernists want to label all books in the library as fiction. If they succeed in convincing readers that all versions of the world presented in books are equal there will be no need to read in order to learn.

Restoration of Platonism in librarianship is necessary if libraries are not to become superfluous, but it would be foolish to advocate a return to some authoritarian form of Platonism: certain postmodernist ideas—such as irreverence towards authority, cultural and linguistic sensitivity, rejection of nationalism, sympathy for the underprivileged and dispossessed—are certainly worth retaining.

Online storage costs have dropped significantly; repositories are now affordable. Standards like the open archives metadata harvesting protocol are now in place; some progress has also been made on the standards for the underlying metadata itself. The thinking about digital preservation over the past five years has advanced to the point where the needs are widely recognized and well defined, the technical approaches at least superficially mapped out, and the need for action is now clear.

The development of free, publicly accessible journal article collections in disciplines such as high-energy physics has demonstrated ways in which the network can change scholarly communication by altering dissemination and access patterns; separately, the development of a series of extraordinary digital works had at least suggested the potential of creative authorship specifically for the digital medium to transform the presentation and transmission of scholarship. A university-based institutional repository is a set of services that a university offers to the members of its community for the management and dissemination of digital materials created by the institution and its community members.

It is most essentially an organizational commitment to the stewardship of these digital materials, including long-term preservation where appropriate, as well as organization and access or distribution. While operational responsibility for these services may reasonably be situated in different organizational units at different universities, an effective institutional repository of necessity represents a collaboration among librarians, information technologists, archives and records mangers, faculty, and university administrators and policymakers. At any given point in time, an institutional repository will be supported by a set of information technologies, but a key part of the services that comprise an institutional repository is the management of technological changes, and the migration of digital content from one set of technologies to the next as part of the organizational commitment to providing repository services. An institutional repository is not simply a fixed set of software and hardware.

While early implementers of institutional repositories have chosen different paths to begin populating their repositories and to build campus community acceptance, support, and participation. A mature and fully realized institutional repository will contain the intellectual works of faculty and students—both research and teaching materials—and also documentation of the activities of the institution itself in the form of records of events and performance and of the ongoing intellectual life of the institution.

At the most basic and fundamental level, an institutional repository is a recognition that the intellectual life and scholarship of our universities will increasingly be represented, documented, and shared in digital form, and that a primary responsibility of our universities is to exercise stewardship over these riches: both to make them available and to preserve them. It is a new channel for structuring the university's contribution to the broader world, and as such invites policy and cultural reassessment of this relationship.

Scholarship and scholarly communication are changing. These changes start with risky and bold acts of individual creativity. They will extend slowly to cultural changes at the disciplinary level and ultimately to new interdisciplinary standards that are expressed in the decisions of institutional tenure and promotion practices. Institutions of higher education have overlooked an opportunity to support the most innovative and creative faculty for at least a decade now, to the detriment of both the faculty members and the institutions themselves. These faculty have been exploring ways in which works of authorship in the new digital medium can enhance teaching and learning and the communication of scholarship; such innovations are essential to keeping scholarship vital and effective, and they must not only be supported but nurtured.

Indeed nurturing these innovations reaches to the core mission of our universities, and to the core values of our universities. A much broader and generally more conservative group of faculty have exploited the Net as a vehicle for sharing their ideas worldwide, whether these ideas are expressed in relatively familiar forms such as digital versions of traditional journal articles or in entirely new forms that begin to map out the future evolution of, for example, the scholarly monograph in the digital medium. This embrace of new dissemination opportunities is also important for what it says about the roles of scholars and universities in society and in a global environment.

Over the past few years, this has ceased to be a reasonable activity for most amateurs; software complexity, security risks, backup requirements, and other problems have generally relegated effective operation of Web sites to professionals who can exploit economies of scale, and who can begin each day with a review of recently issued security patches. However, preservability is an essential prerequisite to any claims to scholarly legitimacy for authoring in the new medium; without being able to claim such works are a permanent part of the scholarly record, it's very hard to argue that they not only deserve but demand full consideration as contributions to scholarship.

Most individual faculty lack the time, resources, or expertise to ensure preservation of their own scholarly work even in the short term, and clearly can't do it in the long term that extends beyond their careers; the long term can only be addressed by an organizationally based strategy. Institutional repositories can address both the near-term questions about continuity of access by providing an environment in which such new works of scholarship can be managed and disseminated—including such basic things as professionally managed systems and systematic backup procedures—and also the longer-term questions about preservation by creating an institutional commitment to such preservation. The revolution in scholarly communications is not limited to the development of new genres of scholarly works that are enabled by the digital medium; even traditional forms such as journal articles now frequently include supplementary datasets and analysis tools.

Scholarship has become data intensive; it is supported and documented by data and tools that complement interpretive works of authorship. Most scientific journals are now accepting what they characterize as "supplementary" materials as part of the publication of traditional journal articles, but it is much less clear what commitments these journals are making to actually integrating these supplementary materials into the permanent record of scholarship in the same way that they maintain the journal articles themselves as a part of that record. Only an institutionally based approach to managing these data resources, which operates in alignment with what the faculty at each individual institution are actually doing, can provide a comprehensive dissemination and preservation mechanism for the data that supports the new scholarship for the digital world.

Journals will move too slowly and too unevenly to manage these resources, and disciplinary data repositories cannot be comprehensive. Institutional repositories can maintain data in addition to authored scholarly works. In this sense, the institutional repository is a complement and a supplement, rather than a substitute, for traditional scholarly publication venues.

Institutional repositories also have roles beyond disseminating and managing the works of individual scholars that are part of the dialog of scholarly communications. Institutional repositories are a place where they can put much of the material that research libraries identify as worth collecting. Finally, at least a few institutions themselves are changing their culture and are making commitments to globally disseminate extensive teaching and learning materials through the Net, or, at a less systematic but still important level, to digitally capture and preserve the many of the events of campus life—symposia, performances, lectures.

Institutional repositories offer a framework for organized stewardship and accessibility of these materials. In short, institutional repositories can facilitate greatly enhanced access to traditional scholarly content by empowering faculty to effectively use the new dissemination capabilities offered by the network. This is also occurring on a disciplinary basis through the development of e-print and preprint servers, at least in some disciplines.

Challenges of Librarianship

For librarianship, the major issues involve what we need to compete and indeed to thrive as a profession in a time when information appears to be ever more readily accessible to information seekers, and when other groups may be seeking to play roles that librarians have traditionally played.

Librarians, together with information technologists and several other professional groups, make up what Andrew Abbott has called "the information professions." Writers on the professions have identified the following representative information professionals: accountants, archivists, librarians, records managers, information systems analysts, management scientists, museum curators, archivists, publishers, and information scientists.

The development and growth of desktop and network computing technologies in the modern workplace have made nearly everyone in an organization dependent on a desktop computer to be productive, computing staffs have grown in size while becoming more active and visible as providers of user assistance and support. In this environment, distinctions among the tasks performed by members of traditionally separate information professions are often expressed in terms of whether the work primarily involves information content (the domain of librarians) or the technologies used to communicate, access, or deliver information content (the domain of technologists). Librarians assist the user in determining where and how to search for information, while technologists provide the means through which the search takes place and ensure that they work properly.

The distinction between content and access technologies may be helpful as a means for allocating support responsibilities within an organization, but it cannot be carried too far as a principle for provision of services. In a network environment where the computer is used for information-seeking and research as well as for other purposes, technologists may find themselves providing content assistance, while librarians may be asked for help with research and access technologies.

Users in need of assistance cannot be expected to make these kinds of distinctions in an environment that is increasingly dependent on networked information and in which it is increasingly difficult to establish clear boundaries between information content and the technologies (such as the world wide web) that provide access to the content and make it useable. Information professionals in both groups may also find the distinction too limiting. A special librarian argues in terms that might well be employed by an information technologist: This distinction is false, misleading, and dangerous.

It is false because content is meaningless until communicated; thus content and access technology are inextricably linked. It is misleading because it suggests that roles may be clearly confined based on this distinction. It is dangerous because it removes from our control some of the most important tools we have to do our fundamental job: connecting people with the information they need. Because of the wide diffusion in the workplace of both information technology and the skills necessary to use and develop it, the lines between content and access technologies are no longer as bright as they might have seemed in the past.

As a result, the boundaries between the information professions are increasingly indistinct, and the content/access distinction can no longer provide the basis for differentiating among them. New relationships among the information professions are developing and will evolve in their common workplace. As they do, it will become increasingly less useful for any group to justify its claims for jurisdiction on earlier understandings about allocations of responsibility. Client relationships are central to success in any profession. Like other information professionals, librarians must know their clients well enough to be able to anticipate their information needs and to exercise judgment on their behalf.

According to Mason, judgment is enhanced by the information professional's "intellectual empathy" with the client's needs and situation. Abbott differentiates among librarians on the basis of what clientele they serve, noting that the work of academic and special librarians has generally been in workplaces shared with other professional groups, such as faculties, attorneys, and physicians. The special librarians claimed that they knew the sources and means to find material that working professionals didn't have the time (and sometimes the ability) to find.

The potentially transformational impacts of the Internet and the world wide web indicate that these sorts of conflicts are likely to intensify as technology becomes more and more important in all workplaces. Some forecast potential conflict between librarians and university faculties as instructional technologies become more important in higher education. The point to be drawn from this is that, at least in academic and special libraries, the relationship between librarians and clients is not purely one of service, but bears resemblance to relationships with other groups in the workplace. Interprofessional conflicts of various types are not a new phenomenon for librarians, nor are they likely to diminish in the future. To compete in the arena of public opinion, a profession must establish a clear identity vis a vis other groups in the workplace.

If a professional is incompetent, organizational function demands that his or her work be done by someone else who is probably not officially qualified to do it. In the jurisdictional system of the workplace, it is the real output of an individual, not his credentialed or noncredentialed status, that matters. These comments certainly resonate in the context of librarianship, where there is much blurring of boundaries between the work of professional and support staff, as evidenced by the difficulties that even regular library users often have in telling who is a librarian and who a clerk on the library staff, and by the comments of library support staff members that their work is no different from that of the higher paid professional staff.

In larger libraries, it is probably more common for non-professionals to do specialized professional-level tasks than it is in smaller libraries, where professional librarians are often required to perform a wide range of professional and nonprofessional tasks. Mark Sandler notes that librarians have generally been able to distinguish themselves from other library workers on the basis of "their links to content and the broader principles underlying information services." Librarians are increasingly unable to maintain control over the qualifications needed to perform library work, in part because information technology has challenged the traditional skill base of librarians.

Distributed computing and access to networked information have blurred the boundaries between librarians' and technologists' established jurisdictions in the information area. Neither librarians nor information technologists have subordinated the other group, and neither group has established intellectual jurisdiction over information provision. Nor is there a formal and stable division of labour. Most writers on the subject of the professions would agree with Talcott Parsons that "the boundaries of the group system we generally call the professions are fluid and indistinct.," as well as with his suggestion that there are several core criteria which distinguish professional work from the work of other occupations.

Library education moved ahead with the accepted practice of its time without first getting its theoretical bearings. As long as the social and economic conditions remained the same, the profession would enjoy some degree of success and acceptance; but if conditions were to change, there was no unified body of theory to provide "conceptual lenses" to look at a completely new set of problems and suggest ways to deal with them. Today, of course, the challenges that widespread diffusion of information technology and access to information pose for users of information and for librarianship as a profession are of much greater magnitude than those posed simply by increases in the quantity of available information.

Library selectors will need to be knowledgeable about many more sources of information; acquisitions librarians will need to know how to choose among such alternative information formats as hard copy, microform, CD-ROM, online, video, and multimedia; reference librarians will play greater roles as information analysts, establishing profiles of individual users' information needs and providing information filters for their clients; catalogers will need to organize access to a new variety of information sources, including materials that the library may not own; and administrators will need to negotiate new kinds of contracts and licenses, maintain different kinds of accounting records, seek alternative sources of support and funding, and be prepared to market library services in the face of new kinds of competition. These changes, all of which arguably stem from the growing role of technology in librarians' work, will expand the knowledge base required to succeed in the profession, and will perhaps alter the list of most desirable traits and characteristics of persons wishing to work as law librarians.

For most professions, the university is the principle seat of training. Academic professional knowledge "legitimates professional work by clarifying its foundations and tracing them to major cultural values." Law librarianship has itself had many distinguished practitioners and leaders who held professional degrees in law, but not in librarianship. Yet, the influence of law-trained librarians on the development of the profession led ultimately to law librarianship's emergence as a clearly identifiable specialization within librarianship, and to the early development of specialized programs in education for law librarianship, many of which continue today. In the late twentieth century, the more likely question in law libraries, as well as other libraries, is whether subject knowledge from other information fields, such as computer science or electrical engineering should be allowed to substitute for the MLS in defining a librarian.

However professional knowledge is obtained by particular individuals, the existence of a body of knowledge is essential for any group wishing to be recognized as a profession. In practice, professionals and clients alike are more likely to be concerned with whether a practitioner has the current skills or competencies needed to serve the client's needs, than with the practitioner's academic knowledge base. The development of highly specialized skills is by itself not enough to establish professional status, because specialization in work is not limited to the professions.

The literature of librarianship frequently focuses on skills or competencies, usually with the aim of identifying the competencies that librarians will need for success in the future. Professional competencies are most closely connected to the special librarian's knowledge base "in the areas of information resources, information access, technology, management, and research," while personal competencies "represent a set of skills, attitudes, and values that enable librarians to work effectively... ."

Professional competencies include such things as expert knowledge of the content of information resources, specialized subject knowledge appropriate for the organization or client, use of appropriate technologies to acquire, organize, and disseminate information, ability to evaluate outcomes and conduct research, and participation as an effective member of the senior management team of the organization. Personal competencies include commitment to excellent service, interest in seeking out challenges and new opportunities, effective communications skills, the ability to both provide leadership and work in teams, personal business skills, flexibility, etc.

Despite changes in how legal information is published, law librarians will continue to acquire, organize, retrieve, preserve, and disseminate information, and assist users in retrieving and using it. Law librarians will need to be versatile, creative, adaptable, flexible, and comfortable with change. They will need to be skilled and articulate instructors, able to work collaboratively within both the library and their larger organization, and able to show equanimity in the face of the frustrations of a rapidly changing work environment. The reports of both professional organizations place their highest emphasis on personal competencies that can be applied in a variety of work settings.

Changes in technology will transform not only the specifics of the librarian's skill set, but the library work environment. In a changing work environment, the successful and effective professionals will be those with the personal skills to adapt and deal with change. Thus, while there may be value in compiling comprehensive lists of professional skills, it is not necessary to insist that all librarians possess the full set, as long as the skills they do possess are underpinned by a shared set of values.

A perspective that places greater emphasis on shared professional values than on lists of skills allows the profession to grow and develop, and to create new relationships with other groups. The elements of professionalism are: fidelity to ethics and integrity; service with competence, dedication, and independence; education as a means for growth and replenishment; civility and respect for authority; and commitment to improving the justice system and advancing the rule of law.

Librarianship remains a female-dominated profession, at least in numbers. On the other hand, the stereotypical information technologist continues to be male. A recent survey of network managers showed found that 17 percent of respondents were women, and that women as a group expressed more dissatisfaction with their salaries and treatment than males. There is also evidence that the number of women preparing for careers in information technology is not rising in pace with the growth of employment opportunities in the area. Because of their common educational qualifications and the fact that they have traditionally worked in easily identifiable workplaces, librarians have generally had few problems maintaining professional identity, even as they became being highly specialized in terms of tasks performed or subject knowledge. Computing professionals, who are also faced with increasing specialization within the profession, have traditionally based their identity in the disciplines of mathematics and engineering.

Computing sits at the crossroads among the central processes of applied mathematics, science, and engineering. The three processes are of equal-and fundamental-importance in the discipline, which is a unique blend of interaction among theory, abstraction, and design. Since 1989, however, networking and communications technologies have become increasingly integrated into all aspects of contemporary business and professional life, and the demand for skilled information technologists has grown exponentially.

Computing has become much less a "back office" operation, and the backgrounds and experiences of those working in the field have become much more heterogeneous. In business, government, and education, many people have attained responsible computing or networking positions with little or no training in the traditional academic disciplines of computing, building new careers upon the discovery that they had the talent for working with technology. Like other professions faced with a rapidly changing work environment, computing professionals have struggled to define the professional knowledge base of a highly specialized and developing field, and to maintain meaningful relationships between academic knowledge and the practice of the profession.

The concern about competencies demonstrates that, like librarians and others, practicing professionals in computing think of the academic base of their profession as remote and divorced from the everyday practice of the field. In librarianship, this concern is often manifested in debates over whether the MLS or an equivalent degree should be required of those working in librarian positions, or whether on-the-job training and appropriate experience, perhaps combined with a subject degree (e.g., in law), can substitute for the professional degree. In computing, however, the issues are less abstract than they might be in librarianship.

For computing professionals and those who hire them, the need to be able to identify, measure, and demonstrate competencies and skills is a matter of immediate practical concern. More than librarians, computing professionals have been forced to deal with rapid and continual changes in their work and in the skills needed to show competency in it. For computing professionals, the competencies and skills need for success in the workplace are most often attained through specialized, short-term training programs, rather than entry-level or advanced degrees.

As a result, the field is characterized by a variety of certification programs, many of which are specialized both by job function and by software product or vendor. Microsoft's network certification programs have risen in popularity as its competing network products have penetrated those markets. Studies show that the educational qualifications of computing professionals are increasing, and changing. A growing percentage of network managers now have advanced degrees in business, or in information systems, as well as, or in place of electrical engineering or computer science degrees.

Employers are looking for technologists who are broadly educated, and who demonstrate a range of skills beyond the technological. All of these developments show a recognition that computing support in an organization is no longer a back office operation, and that information technologists are fully conscious of their roles as active intermediaries involved both in making sure that technology is functional and in helping clients use technology effectively. Librarians and information technologists both face challenging and uncertain futures, in part because of the pace of change in the information environment, and in part because ready access to information technology has blurred the traditional distinctions among areas of jurisdiction in the workplace. Continuing development of the access technologies that provide the means for finding information will continue to affect and change the librarian's work, and require more of the librarian's attention and understanding.

In this environment, the librarian's professional grounding in content expertise will remain important, but in a new sense. There is now and will be a growing need for professionals who can sift and sort through information, not only to locate pieces of information, but to put those pieces into context, and to weigh and compare different items, identify, authenticate and validate them. Librarians and technologists alike should be thinking more about context and point of view than about content and access as separate concepts.

The ability to provide context to the client's process of information seeking will be key to the future of the information professions, but context is a product of both content and access, and can be provided only through consideration and understanding of both elements. Complexity is inherent in most information-seeking, resulting from both the abundance of content and the crude methods available to access it.

It is unnecessary to say much about the problems posed by the sheer masses of potentially useful information available on any topic, the difficulties in knowing whether any search has found everything that might be useful, or the problems involved in weighing and authenticating what is found. Historically, these all are reasons for the development and endurance of the library as an institution and librarianship as a profession.

For many, the promise of the digital library lies in its capacity to provide integrated access to material that is of less permanent value and less archival in nature than the usual library holdings: Seen from this new perspective, the digital library is a seamless blend of the conventional archive of current or historically important information and knowledge, along with ephemeral material such as drafts, notes, memoranda and files of ongoing activity. The potential for blending digitally-formatted information of various types provides the impetus for the current interest of corporations (and librarians) in "knowledge management."

The idea of knowledge management, the "process of capturing a company's collective expertise wherever it resides—in databases, on paper, or in people's heads—and distributing it to wherever it can help produce the biggest payoff," is made possible because information of all sorts can be collected, stored, and distributed in a common digital format. Of course, this also adds to the rapid growth in the amount of information potentially available for any situation, leaving "knowledge workers feeling both overwhelmed by information and fearful that they're missing important details."

But such purely technological solutions to the problem rely on the proposition that access technologies can be readily separated from content. As a result, they too readily dismiss the importance of "human factors" in interface design, revealing both too much faith in the abilities of intelligent interfaces to overcome the difficulties and complexities of the information-seeking process and too little understanding of the actual needs of human information seekers, who require context to be successful in their quest. Before relying too heavily on automated devices to navigate through masses of digitized personal and archival research information, it is worth examining the computing industry's track record for developing interface and other access software.

It has become commonplace to observe that the usual effect of software upgrades and improvements is to provide additional features and options at the cost of increased complexity in the software interface. Microsoft's introduction of Windows '95 was greeted in the technology, corporate, and general media with a chorus of concern about the value of software upgrades, not only because of their cost and disruption, but because for most users upgrades are more likely to complicate their normal work than to add useful functionality. The growing complexities of the information and research environments will demand increasingly powerful and sophisticated interfaces and research tools.

Access technologies are indeed the "means" to the information content at the end of the search, but means of access are vital to the success of the search process. And librarians may pay too little attention to them. There was a time at the last turn of the century, when librarians were not only guardians of information, but were the primary creators of indexes and other finding tools used by readers to locate information. Somewhere along the line, however, librarians gradually gave up responsibility for that work, first to the publishing industry and now to information technologists.

If librarians truly are experts in the human elements of the information-seeking process, as well as in the content of information, we need to become more involved in tool-building in order to be sure that content is accessible in ways that are meaningful to users. This will require significantly greater commitment to the development of skills in access technologies and the acknowledgment that those skills are as important for librarians as for technologists. Content expertise alone will be increasingly less useful without the "deeper" technological proficiencies needed to provide effective access to information and help users work with it in a variety of formats.

The need to develop greater proficiencies in technology does not mean that librarians should abandon the roots of their own profession. Rather, it is essential to revisit those roots and to consider what might already have been forgotten as librarians have concentrated on gaining professional recognition and dealing with the challenges of the information environment. Librarianship developed as a service-oriented, client-centered profession: one in which meeting the client's needs as the client sees them has been of more importance than the expertise of the professional.

This perspective has differentiated librarianship from other professions, such as law or medicine. Librarians must also consider the effects of their growing roles as managers within their organizations. Performance of the skills associated with professional work is a highly visible manifestation of professional status. Yet, as larger libraries have become more complex organizations and have placed a greater weight on managerial skills, much apparently professional library work is performed by non-librarians.

One of the greatest democratic acts of our culture was to recognize information and knowledge as public goods. Today, our libraries are the keepers of the "commons of knowledge" that is so vital a part of our society. Libraries are the only institutions that attempt to provide a view of the whole of our society's information resources without bias. Libraries carry the good and the bad, the right and the wrong, the proven and the dubious. And they've generally had little competition - until recently, information wasn't a hot product. But now, suddenly, information is the "product of the 90's."

Normally cautious investors seem unable to resist the media hype that has arisen from the idea of the "information highway." There is a frightening amount of financial activity taking place around non-existant products and a rather vague promise of future markets. There is an inherent conflict between information as a "hot product" and information as a "public good." It manifested in the proposed changes to the copyright law. At the hearings held last fall for public testimony on the proposed changes, emphasis was clearly on intellectual property as product.

Electronic information can be copied without losing any quality. And it can be copied quickly and in large numbers of copies. To a manufacturer, this means a high profit margin. But it also means that it can be copied and distributed by people with inexpensive equipment and very little skill. So information, the product, is hard to protect. One of the results of this is that the tendency is not to sell copies, but to lease them. You don't buy software, you enter into a license for it. This helps the original manufacturer keep control over the product. In the world of electronic documents, leasing, rather than selling, is already the norm. This is a big change for libraries.

The library of today still based on hardcopy/print model. Libraries buy print materials, organize them, and lend them to the public. But libraries have already have some experience with electronic resources. These have primarily been finding tools, notably citations to hardcopy documents. What is changing is that we are now talking about actual end product, the document itself, being electronic.

Some systems provide the full text of published articles; increasingly, government documents are being made available electronically, and libraries are accessing the Internet, which is an entirely new type of information resource. Copyright law was originally drafted in a world where intellectual property was always embodied in a physical form, such as a book or journal. Copyright was a Congressional act to create a balance between the creators of intellectual property and public good. Licensers are in the business of providing their information for revenue, and are under no obligation to consider public good.

They exist not a service to the public, but as a business. This is a big change in position of library in information "food chain." There was a line from the creator to the publisher to the library and finally to the public. In this case, the library is the public interface on all information, and is the guarantee of public access. The new model goes from the creator to the publisher to the public - because the publisher provides the interface to the electronic documents.

The library is reduced to a pass-through point, both for someone else's information, but also for the organization and control of the information. This is not all that different to having a telephone or television in the library - patrons are accessing a service that would be the same whether or not the library existed. Libraries have always been distributors of other people's information, but through their activities they transformed the many voices in the information world into a coherent view of the full range of ancient and modern thought.

Few libraries can even try to collect "everything," so libraries must select information based on its quality and suitability to the library's mission. This isn't always possible inthe presentation of electronic works. For example, most libraries don't select hard core porn, but it will be part of their offerings when they link to the Internet. Online systems might not reflect needs of the library's users.

Index